Reactive Streams in Java

Concurrency with RxJava, Reactor, and Akka Streams

Adam L. Davis

Apress®

Reactive Streams in Java: Concurrency with RxJava, Reactor,
and Akka Streams

Adam L. Davis
Oviedo, FL, USA

ISBN-13 (pbk): 978-1-4842-4175-2 ISBN-13 (electronic): 978-1-4842-4176-9
https://doi.org/10.1007/978-1-4842-4176-9

Library of Congress Control Number: 2018965180

Managing Director, Apress Media LLC: Welmoed Spahr
Acquisitions Editor: Steve Anglin
Development Editor: Matthew Moodie
Coordinating Editor: Mark Powers

Cover designed by eStudioCalamar

Cover image designed by Freepik (www.freepik.com)

Distributed to the book trade worldwide by Springer Science+Business Media New York, 233 Spring Street, 6th Floor, New York, NY 10013. Phone 1-800-SPRINGER, fax (201) 348-4505, e-mail orders-ny@springer-sbm.com, or visit www.springeronline.com. Apress Media, LLC is a California LLC and the sole member (owner) is Springer Science + Business Media Finance Inc (SSBM Finance Inc). SSBM Finance Inc is a **Delaware** corporation.

For information on translations, please e-mail editorial@apress.com; for reprint, paperback, or audio rights, please email bookpermissions@springernature.com.

Apress titles may be purchased in bulk for academic, corporate, or promotional use. eBook versions and licenses are also available for most titles. For more information, reference our Print and eBook Bulk Sales web page at http://www.apress.com/bulk-sales.

Any source code or other supplementary material referenced by the author in this book is available to readers on GitHub via the book's product page, located at www.apress.com/9781484241752. For more detailed information, please visit http://www.apress.com/source-code.

Printed on acid-free paper

Table of Contents

About the Author

Adam L. Davis (@adamldavis) makes software. He's spent many years developing in Java (since Java 1.2) and has enjoyed using Spring and Hibernate. Since 2006 he's been using Groovy and Grails in addition to Java to create SaaS web applications that help track finances for large institutions (among other things). Adam has a master's and a bachelor's degree in computer science from Georgia Tech. For more, visit http://adamldavis.com.

About the Technical Reviewer

Manuel Jordan Elera is an autodidactic developer and researcher who enjoys learning new technologies for his own experiments and creating new integrations. Manuel won the Springy Award – Community Champion and Spring Champion 2013. In his little free time, he reads the Bible and composes music on his guitar. Manuel is known as dr_pompeii. He has tech reviewed numerous books for Apress, including *Pro Spring, 4th Edition* (2014); *Practical Spring LDAP* (2013); *Pro JPA 2, Second Edition* (2013); and *Pro Spring Security* (2013). Read his 13 detailed tutorials about many Spring technologies, contact him through his blog at `www.manueljordanelera.blogspot.com`, and follow him on his Twitter account, `@dr_pompeii`.

Preface

Who Is the Target Audience?

This book is intended for Java developers of beginning or intermediate skill who wish to learn more about reactive programming. If you are still reading this, then that probably means you!

Why You Should Read This Book

You should read this book to learn the basic of reactive programming with Reactive Streams and understand what they are good for, when they should be used, and the principles behind them. This book uses straightforward examples and introduces concepts gradually so as not to overwhelm the reader. It will refer to existing models of concurrency from time to time only as reference points and will not assume any advanced knowledge on the topic.

After reading this book, you should have a firm understanding of Reactive Streams, including three different implementations, and how to integrate them into real software projects. You will understand when to use Reactive Streams, how to write tests, and how to build a whole project.

What Is Not in This Book

This book assumes you have a basic background of programming in Java, so it will not cover the basics.

For more of an introduction on basic Java concepts, please check out my other books: *Modern Programming Made Easy, Modern Java, and What's New in Java 8.*

CHAPTER 1

Introduction to Reactive Streams

Reactive Streams is an initiative to provide a standard for asynchronous stream processing with non-blocking back pressure. This encompasses efforts aimed at runtime environments (JVM and JavaScript) as well as network protocols.

—reactive-streams.org

At their core, Reactive Streams are an effort to provide highly responsive applications able to handle many requests per second with the ability to manage backpressure (the ability to skip or queue data that is coming too fast to be processed). Asynchronous means processing can take place in many threads, without stopping to read data from a file or a web request for example. Although many implementations already exist for asynchronous processing, such as Java's Future, CompletableFuture, and parallel streams, most of them do not have standard support for asynchronous handling of backpressure.

Reactive Streams are a unifying standard that abstracts existing methods of concurrency. Also, by having one standard, different Reactive Streams implementations can interoperate in one application.

© Adam L. Davis 2019
A. L. Davis, *Reactive Streams in Java*, https://doi.org/10.1007/978-1-4842-4176-9_1

Java 9+

Java 9 was an important release of Java and includes Project Jigsaw which represents a huge restructuring of the core JDK (Java Development Kit) as well as a new and improved way of defining code dependencies. This provides compile-time errors when dependencies are missing as opposed to runtime errors, which is a vast improvement for software development efficiency. Java 9 also introduced a unified interface for Reactive Streams.

Java 9 includes the following key features:

- Language updates

- Support for Reactive Streams

- Modularity (Project Jigsaw)

- Java REPL (jshell)

For the purposes of this book, we will focus on the second item and cover what Reactive Streams are and how they should be used. Although at the time of writing this is not the case, all implementations of Reactive Streams in Java are expected to implement the Java 9 API in the near future. We will cover changes in Java 10 and 11 in how they affect our code going forward.

Flow

Support for Reactive Streams has been added to the JDK. Several interfaces have been added in the `java.util.concurrent.Flow` class:

- `Publisher<T>`: A producer of items (and related control messages) received by Subscribers

- `Subscriber<T>`: A receiver of messages

- `Processor<T,R>`: A component that acts as both a `Subscriber` and `Publisher`

- `Subscription`: Message control linking a Publisher and Subscriber

No actual implementation is included in the JDK; however, several implementations already exist. Current notable implementations of the Reactive Streams specification on the Java virtual machine (JVM) are Project Reactor (which is integrated in Spring 5), Akka Streams, and RxJava, all of which we will cover in this book.

Code for This Book

The code examples used in this book are available on my repository on GitHub. Feel free to download this code which is open source and play around with it. If you do not already have a GitHub account, you can create one completely for free. It helps to have Git installed on your own machine. Then use the `git clone` command, as specified on the GitHub landing page, and use whatever Integrated Development Environment (IDE) you feel is compatible with you – even a text editor will do.

CHAPTER 2

Existing Models of Concurrency in Java

As multicore processors become more and more standard, different models of concurrent programming have become more popular in Java. Although the core model of concurrency in Java is the Thread, multiple levels of abstraction have been built to enable simpler development.

Each of these models has a different approach toward protecting values from being modified by more than one thread at one time as we will cover in this chapter.

Prominent Models for Concurrency

There are several tried and true models of concurrency in Java and the JVM. Over time, higher level models have been introduced to make concurrency simpler. Some of these models are the following:

- Synchronize and suffer (using `synchronize` keyword in Java)

- Futures and the ExecutorService

- Software transactional memory (STM) (Clojure)

- Actor-based model (Akka)

- Reactive Streams (RxJava, Reactor, etc.)

© Adam L. Davis 2019
A. L. Davis, *Reactive Streams in Java*, https://doi.org/10.1007/978-1-4842-4176-9_2

Synchronize in Java

The original style of concurrent programming in Java involves using the `synchronized` keyword whenever shared resources are modified. The runtime behavior of this style of programming is very unpredictable and difficult to test. You must deal with the following problems:

- No warnings or errors are given at compile time.

- Deadlocks can occur if you're not careful.

- It's very difficult to make sure you've done everything right, and errors can occur randomly.

In conclusion, the `synchronize` keyword is too low level to use (just don't use it!).[1]

Java Futures

You may have heard of the `java.util.concurrent.Future` interface in Java. Maybe you've even used it. This interface was added in Java 1.5, and it holds the result of an asynchronous computation. It contains methods to check if the asynchronous computation is complete or still in progress, to wait for the completion of the computation, to block the call until the completion of the computation (with optional timeout), and to retrieve the result of the computation.

---

[1] I would also categorize the `volatile` keyword similarly in that it is a low-level construct that should be avoided.

Drawbacks of the Future Interface

There are tons of problems with this interface:

- When using Java's Future, we tend to loop on isDone(), which ties up the thread, or call get() which blocks the thread completely.

- ExecutorService#submit(...) is used the most (which returns a Future with a get() method that returns null).

- Generally when "going asynchronous", we don't care about the result, or we want to do something with the result (thus we want something like a continuation).

- We need a callback – removes the need for polling (isDone) and blocking. (Guava's ListenableFuture provides this.)

- Asynchronous methods should always return void.

For these reasons, if you do any concurrent programming, you should use the CompletableFuture introduced in Java 8 (which is covered next), the Java 7 concurrency API (ForkJoinPool and ForkJoinTask), or another concurrency framework.

CompletableFuture

The CompletableFuture<T> implements the Future<T> interface as well as a CompletionStage<T> interface that fills in many of the deficiencies of Future<T>. These methods follow the functional style, allowing the developer to chain method calls rather than declaring a step-by-step process.

CompletionStage includes the following methods (generic types omitted for brevity) which each have the return type of CompletionStage to allow chaining:

- acceptEither(CompletionStage, Consumer): Executes the given consumer when either this stage (the current Future) or the given stage completes.

- applyToEither(CompletionStage, Function): Similar to acceptEither but uses a Function to convert a value into another value.

- exceptionally(Function): If the stage throws an exception, the given function is given the exception to process and return a value.

- handle(BiFunction): Uses the given function to handle both the success and failure conditions and returns a value.

- runAfterBoth(CompletionStage, Runnable): Runs the given Runnable after both this stage (the current Future) and the given stage complete.

- runAfterEither(CompletionStage, Runnable): Similar to acceptEither except using a Runnable.

- thenAccept(Consumer): Runs the given consumer after this stage (the current Future) completes normally. This is similar to "then" in Promise models of concurrency if you're familiar with Promises.

- `thenAcceptBoth(CompletionStage, BiConsumer)`:
  Runs the given biconsumer with both outputs after
  both this stage (the current Future) and the given stage
  complete normally.

- `thenApply(Function)`: Transforms a value using the
  given function after the stage completes normally.

- `thenCombine(CompletionStage, BiFunction)`:
  Transforms two values using the given function after
  both stages complete normally.

- `thenRun(Runnable)`: Runs the given `Runnable` after this
  stage completes.

- `whenComplete(BiConsumer)`: Uses the given consumer
  to handle both the success and failure conditions.

Asynchronous versions of these methods are also available with
"Async" added to the method name. For the "Async" versions, the
standard execution model of the given Future will be used instead of the
current Thread.

You can create an instance using any of the following static methods
on `CompletableFuture`:

- `CompletableFuture completedFuture(value)`:
  Returns a new `CompletableFuture` that is already
  completed with the given value.

- `CompletableFuture runAsync(Runnable)`: Returns
  a new `CompletableFuture` that is asynchronously
  completed by a task running in the `ForkJoinPool.`
  `commonPool()`.

- `CompletableFuture runAsync(Runnable, Executor)`: Returns a new `CompletableFuture` that is asynchronously completed by a task running in the given executor after it runs the given action.

- `CompletableFuture supplyAsync(Supplier)`: Returns a new `CompletableFuture` that is asynchronously completed by a task running in the `ForkJoinPool. commonPool()` with the value obtained by calling the given `Supplier`.

For more details, please see the <u>documentation</u>.

STM in Clojure

Java doesn't have great support for concurrency built-in. Other languages for the JVM (Java virtual machine), like Scala and Clojure, have been built from the ground up with concurrency in mind. However, we can use the concurrency models from Scala and Clojure straight in Java.

STM (<u>software transactional memory</u>) results in a separation of state and identity. For example, the stock price at a given time is immutable. In STM you must use a transaction to modify anything. We can include the Clojure jars and use them within Java. For example, in the following code, `referenceToAmount` can only be modified inside of a transaction:

```
import clojure.lang.*;
Ref referenceToAmount;
LockingTransaction.runInTransaction(new Callable() {
     referenceToAmount.set(value);
});
```

Now you will get an error if you try to modify the `Ref` outside of a transaction. This makes concurrent programming easier because modifying data outside of a synchronized block is impossible.

Actors

The Scala-based actor framework Akka can also be used from Java.
Akka is also used by the Play Framework. It includes the concept of Actors.
Actors can receive and process messages and are guaranteed to receive
messages sent to them. They process each message one at a time so their
state is shielded from the rest of the system.

The following code shows a simple example using the Akka framework
with one Actor:

```java
import akka.actor.*;
public class XActor extends UntypedActor {
  public void onReceive(Object message) throws Exception {
    if (message instanceof String)
      System.out.println((String) message);
  }
}
  public static void main(String... args) {
    ActorSystem system = ActorSystem.create("MySystem");
    ActorRef actor = system.actorOf(new Props(XActor.class),
                  "actor");
    // the message could be anything implementing Serializable
    actor.tell("Message String");
}
```

An Actor conceptually runs in a dedicated thread, so it can only do
one thing at a time. This makes concurrency much easier to implement.
Messages are passed around to Actors and wait in a queue until the
given Actor is ready to process it. A message can be any Serializable
object.

Groovy GPars

It's worth noting that the Actor and STM concurrency patterns are not limited to Scala and Clojure.

Groovy's GPars library implements these patterns as well and is also usable from Java. It also has Domain Specific Languages (DSLs) that wrap the JSR-166 features of Java, such as the Fork-Join framework, making them easier to use.

You can use GPars to do filter, map, and reduce an array in the following way:

```
GParsPool.withPool {
  // a map-reduce functional style (students is a Collection)
  def bestGpa = students.parallel
    .filter{ s -> s.graduationYear == 2017 }
    .map{ s -> s.gpa }
    .max()
}
```

In this example, Student is a class with a `graduationYear` and gpa. This code finds the highest GPA for 2017. The static method `GParsPool.withPool` takes in a closure and augments any Collection with several methods (using Groovy's category mechanism). The parallel method actually creates a `ParallelArray` (JSR-166) from the given Collection and uses it with a thin wrapper around it.

Reactive Streams

Reactive Streams provide an abstraction for highly concurrent, asynchronous applications with support for backpressure.

While they can be used along with any of the preceding models of concurrency, they attempt to provide enough functionality to be fully sufficient for any implementation (over and above the other

models of concurrency). However, since they run in a multithreaded
way, you must ensure thread safety in your code if you modify
shared state. Try to avoid using other methods (e.g., using a
`LockingTransaction` or synchronize block) and instead stay within
the Reactive Streams model. Reactive Streams use the concepts of
publisher and subscriber, along with various strategies for backpressure
to model concurrency. We will cover these concepts.

- A publisher emits events at some rate.

- A subscriber observes those events on possibly a
  different thread and does something with them.

- Some frameworks use other words (such as Source
  and Sink) to mean the same thing as publisher and
  subscriber.

As we will see, many Reactive Streams frameworks allow
interoperation with other existing models of concurrency, such as futures,
to allow a smooth transition between the two.

CHAPTER 3

Common Concepts

Every Reactive Streams framework uses common concepts forming the backbone of reactive streams. You can use method chaining to perform complex conversions of streams in a simple and terse syntax once you know the function of standard methods like filter, map, delay, and buffer.

This chapter attempts to illustrate the most important of these concepts. It does not cover all available methods.

Streams

The word *Observable* is used to mean a reactive stream of data. Although Observable is a type in RxJava, this and the other Reactive Streams libraries have other types, such as *Flux* in Reactor and *Source* in Akka Streams, that represent *streams of data*. Everything in Reactive Streams starts with a stream.

Hot and Cold

When you begin using Reactive Streams, you need to master the concept of hot vs. cold Observables. It's not always obvious which type you are dealing with and the interactions between them cause problems.

A hot Observable is one that cannot be repeated. It starts creating data immediately regardless of whether it has subscribers. Typically it involves interacting with data from the outside world such as mouse inputs, data readings, or web requests.

© Adam L. Davis 2019
A. L. Davis, *Reactive Streams in Java*, https://doi.org/10.1007/978-1-4842-4176-9_3

A cold Observable is one that can be repeated and does not start until subscribed to. This could be things like a range, file data, or a cached recording of data from a hot Observable.

Hot Observables typically are candidates for using backpressure flow control strategies such as throttling, buffers, or windows.

Backpressure

Backpressure is what happens when there are too many events/data in a stream than the downstream can handle. As an analogy, think of what happens in some cities at rush hour when traffic grinds to a halt – or when subway trains are filled to capacity. When this happens in your application, it can cause big problems like OutOfMemory exceptions or starved threads and timeouts. Backpressure strategies help you deal with these problems proactively to avoid these problems.

There are multiple backpressure strategies, but the main ones are throttling, windows, buffers, and dropping. The simplest to understand is dropping: you simply drop the items above what can be handled (using some criteria such as oldest or newest). The other strategies (throttling, windows, and buffers) are also listed in this chapter.

Filter

Filter takes only those elements that match a given predicate.

Any/All

Any returns a Boolean value which is true if any elements in the stream match the given predicate. *All* returns true if all the elements match. These two only make sense for terminating (noninfinite) streams.

Map

Map converts data from one form into another. This is useful for any basic operations on data elements.

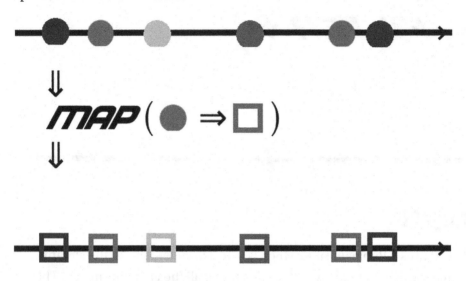

FlatMap/ConcatMap

FlatMap maps data from one form into a stream of other forms and then weaves the resulting streams together. This is useful when you want to convert one data stream into a new stream based on the results of substreams. For example, you might want to convert a stream of sports teams into a stream of all the players of those teams.

ConcatMap is very similar, but preserves the ordering of the incoming streams, whereas flatMap eagerly subscribes to each new stream and merges the results in the order in which they arrive.

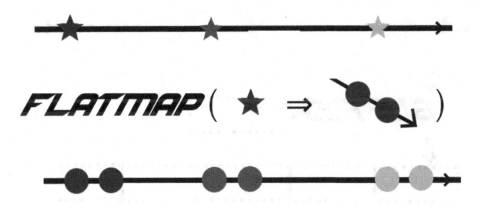

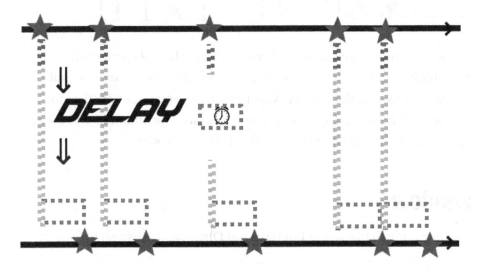

Delay

This method delays data for a fixed amount of time.

Buffer

Buffer keeps data over some time period and sticks it in a list, then observes each list.

19

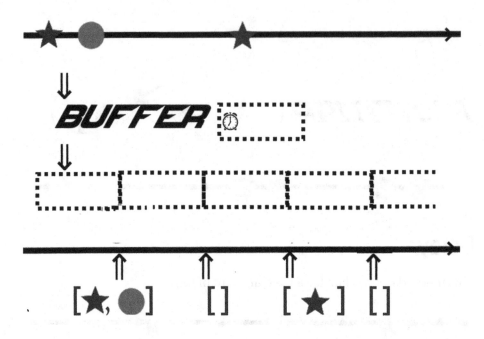

Buffer is also a backpressure strategy that caches all elements from a stream if too many elements were produced than the subscriber could handle. In this case the buffer is kept in memory and does not affect the data type of the stream. If buffer is used, you have the option of *dropping* or ignoring any elements above the buffer's maximum size.

Window

Window is much like buffer but results in Observables instead of lists.

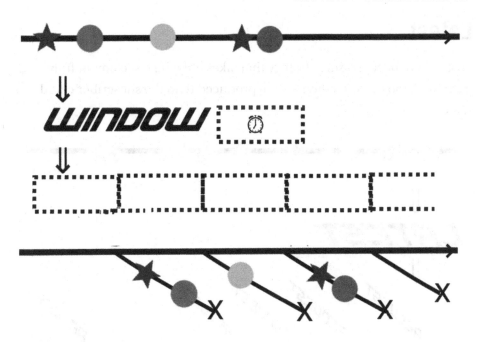

Take While

Take while (takeWhile) takes all elements while some condition is true, then ends the stream when it is false. There is usually also a take(n) method which takes a certain number of elements before ending the stream.

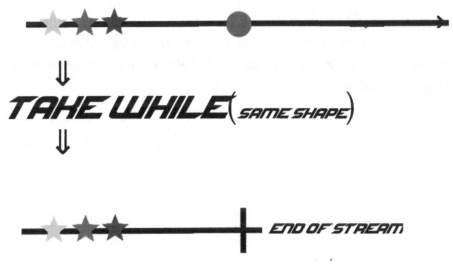

Latest

"Latest" is a backpressure strategy that takes only the last element from a stream if too many elements were produced than the subscriber could handle.

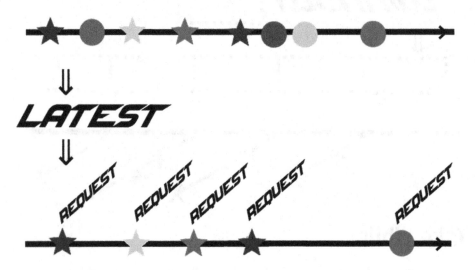

Debounce

Debounce is useful for noisy streams, for example, a text input or other user inputs, when you only want elements after the stream was quiet for some period of time. It gives you only the last element if the stream is silent for a given duration.

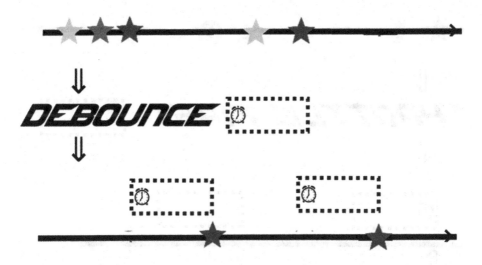

Although Reactor does not seem to have "debounce", it can be approximated using *sampleTimeout*. For example, the following would be equivalent to debounce of one second:

```
flux.sampleTimeout(x ->
        Mono.just(0).delayElement(
                Duration.of(1, ChronoUnit.SECONDS)))
```

Throttle First

Throttle first (throttleFirst in RxJava) drops any elements from the stream (after the first element emitted) for some given duration. Throttle last is very similar only emitting the last element emitted during the time period instead of the first. Reactor has similar methods, *sample* and *sampleFirst*. Akka Streams has a similar method named *throttle*.

CHAPTER 4

RxJava

RxJava is the open source library for reactive programming that is part of the ReactiveX project. ReactiveX includes implementations in several different languages including RxJS, RxRuby, RxSwift, RxPHP, RxGroovy, and many more.

    RxJava 2 was rebuilt to be compatible with the Reactive Streams specification and is preferable to RxJava 1.x since it is scheduled for end-of-life. There were many changes from version 1 to 2 that could be confusing. To avoid confusion we will focus on RxJava 2.

Getting Started

First, create a new project with sources under src/main/java/ and a "pom. xml" if using Maven or a "build.gradle" file if using Gradle.

    If you have a <u>Maven</u> build, add the following to your pom file:

```
<dependency>
  <groupId>io.reactivex.rxjava2</groupId>
  <artifactId>rxjava</artifactId>
  <version>2.2.2</version>
</dependency>
```

    For <u>Gradle</u> builds, add the following to your Gradle build file's dependencies:

```
compile 'io.reactivex.rxjava2:rxjava:2.2.2'
```

© Adam L. Davis 2019
A. L. Davis, *Reactive Streams in Java*, https://doi.org/10.1007/978-1-4842-4176-9_4

Next, create a new class file with the following imports:

```
import io.reactivex.*;
import io.reactivex.schedulers.*;
import io.reactivex.functions.*;
import org.reactivestreams.Publisher;
import org.reactivestreams.Subscriber;
import org.reactivestreams.Subscription;
import java.util.*;
import java.io.*;
```

Flowable

The basic entry class in RxJava is `io.reactivex.Flowable<T>` (which is roughly equivalent to `io.reactivex.Observable<T>`). It implements the Reactive Streams pattern (Publisher) and offers factory methods, intermediate operators, and the ability to consume reactive dataflows.

The following example demonstrates using RxJava to do a simple calculation on a range of numbers:

```
public static List doSquares() {
        List squares = new ArrayList();
        Flowable.range(1, 64) //1
          .observeOn(Schedulers.computation()) //2
          .map(v -> v * v) //3
          .blockingSubscribe(squares::add); //4
        return squares;
}
```

1. Create a range from 1 to 64.

2. Call the method observeOn to determine which
    Scheduler to use. This determines on which Thread
    or Threads the flow will run. The Scheduler returned
    from "computation()" takes advantage of all
    available processors when possible.

3. The map method transforms each value. In this case
    we calculate the square.

4. Finally, we initiate the flow by calling a "subscribe"
    method. In this case, blockingSubscribe blocks
    until the entire flow has completed, and we add
    each value to the "squares" List. This means that
    the squares list will be populated before the return
    statement. Otherwise the flow would run on a
    different thread and the values in the squares list
    would be unpredictable at any given time.

The resulting List will have the values of squares of the numbers
from 1 to 64: 1, 4, 9, 16, 25, 36, 49, ..., 4096.

Parallel Computing

If you tie a Flowable to one Scheduler as in the previous example, it would
run in succession, not in parallel. To run each calculation in parallel, you
could use flatMap to break out each calculation into a separate Flowable
as follows:

```
public static List doParallelSquares() {
        List squares = new ArrayList();
        Flowable.range(1, 64)
          .flatMap(v -> //1
```

```
        Flowable.just(v)
        .subscribeOn(Schedulers.computation())
        .map(w -> w * w)
    )
    .doOnError(ex -> ex.printStackTrace()) //2
    .doOnComplete(() ->
        System.out.println("Completed")) //3
    .blockingSubscribe(squares::add);

    return squares;
}
```

1. Call `flatMap` with a lambda expression that takes in a value and returns another Flowable. The Flowable. just(…) method takes in any number of objects and returns a Flowable that will emit those objects and then complete.

2. Call `doOnError` to handle errors that occur.

3. Call `doOnComplete` to execute something after a Flowable has completed. This is only possible for Flowables that have clear endings, such as ranges. The resulting List will have the same values as the previous example, but since we used flatMap, the resulting values will not necessarily be in the same order.

Schedulers

For some heavy computations, you may want to run them in the background while rendering the result in a separate thread so as not to block the UI or rendering thread. For this case, you can use the `subscribeOn` method with one Scheduler and the `observeOn` method with a different Scheduler.

```
public static void runComputation() throws Exception {
        Flowable<String> source = Flowable.fromCallable(
        () -> { //1
                Thread.sleep(1000);
                return "Done";
        });
        source.doOnComplete(
        () ->           System.out.println("Completed
                        runComputation"));
        Flowable<String> background =
                source.subscribeOn(Schedulers.io()); //2

        Flowable<String> foreground =
                background.observeOn(Schedulers.single()); //3

        foreground.subscribe(System.out::println,
                Throwable::printStackTrace); //4
}
```

1. Create a new Flowable from a Callable (functional
    interface (SAM) which simply returns a value).

2. Run the Flowable using the "IO" Scheduler. This
    Scheduler uses a cached thread pool which is good
    for I/O (e.g., reading and writing to disk or network
    transfers).

3. Observe the results of the Flowable using a single-
    threaded Scheduler.

4. Finally, subscribe to the resulting foreground
    Flowable to initiate the flow and print the results to
    standard out. The result of calling runComputation()
    will be "Done" printed after one second.

Publishers

For nontrivial problems, you might need to create your own Publisher. You would only do this if you wanted fine control over the request/ response nature of Reactive Streams, and it is not necessary to use RxJava.

For the following example, imagine you want to write to a file or read from a file using a custom Publisher in RxJava.

First, we write a range of numbers to a file using the following method:

```
public static void writeFile(File file) {
  try (PrintWriter pw = new PrintWriter(file)) {
    Flowable.range(1, 100)
        .observeOn(Schedulers.newThread())
        .blockingSubscribe(pw::println);
  } catch (FileNotFoundException e) {
    e.printStackTrace();
  }
}
```

Here we use a try-with-resources block and blockingSubscribe to write the range to the file.

Second, we want to read from a file. In this example, the contents of a file are printed to standard out using the "IO" Scheduler:

```
public static void readFile(File file) {
  try (final BufferedReader br = new BufferedReader(
        new FileReader(file))) {
    Flowable<String> flow = Flowable.fromPublisher(
        new FilePublisher(br));
    flow.observeOn(Schedulers.io())
        .blockingSubscribe(System.out::println);
```

```
} catch (IOException e) {
  e.printStackTrace();
}
}
```

A Publisher implements the subscribe method that takes a Subscriber. The Subscriber interface has several methods on it, the first of which to call is onSubscribe(Subscription). To implement backpressure in Reactive Streams, the Subscription interface was created which has only two methods, request(n) for requesting the next n elements and cancel for canceling the subscription.

```
static class FilePublisher implements Publisher<String> {
 BufferedReader reader;
 public FilePublisher(BufferedReader reader)
       { this.reader = reader; }
 @Override
 public void subscribe(Subscriber<? super String> subscriber){
  subscriber.onSubscribe(
       new FilePublisherSubscription(this, subscriber));
 }
 public String readLine() throws IOException {
  return reader.readLine();
 }
}
static class FilePublisherSubscription
       implements Subscription {
 FilePublisher publisher;
 Subscriber<? super String> subscriber;
 public FilePublisherSubscription( FilePublisher publisher,
       Subscriber<? super String> subscriber) {
```

```
 this.publisher = publisher;
 this.subscriber = subscriber;
 }
@Override
public void request(long n) {
 try {
  String line;
  for (int i = 0; i < n && publisher != null
     && (line = publisher.readLine()) != null; i++) {
   if (subscriber != null) subscriber.onNext(line);
  }
 } catch (IOException ex) {
  subscriber.onError(ex);
 }
  subscriber.onComplete();
 }
@Override
public void cancel() {
 publisher = null;
 }
}
```

This example shows how you might implement a Publisher for reading files including backpressure support. A similar approach could be used for any Publisher/Subscription implementation.

Now when we call readFile(File) with a File object, the contents of the file will be read and printed out. The same effect could also be achieved using RxJava in the following way:

```
Single<BufferedReader> readerSingle = Single.just(file) //1
        .observeOn(Schedulers.io()) //2
       .map(FileReader::new)
       .map(BufferedReader::new); //3
```

```
Flowable<String> flowable =
    readerSingle.flatMapPublisher(reader -> //4
        Flowable.fromIterable( //5
                () ->
        Stream.generate(readLineSupplier(reader)).iterator()
    ).takeWhile(line -> !"EOF".equals(line))); //6
flowable
        .doOnNext(it -> System.out.println("thread="
        + Thread.currentThread().getName())) //7
    .doOnError(ex -> ex.printStackTrace())
    .blockingSubscribe(System.out::println); //8
```

1. Single is much like an Observable that can only emit one element. Here we create an instance from the file parameter.

2. We use Schedulers.io() since we're reading a file.

3. Next, we use the constructor reference syntax to instantiate a FileReader and BufferedReader from the original file.

4. Here we use the flatMapPublisher method which is a variant of flatMap that only exists on a "Single" and returns a Flowable.

5. We create a new Flowable using "fromIterable" that will read each line of the file using the BufferedReader. We use "Stream.generate" since it repeatably calls the given supplier given by the "readLineSupplier" method.

6. When readLine() returns null, the file is done being read, but an Iterator cannot supply null so we use "EOF" instead. We use that as the predicate for "takeWhile" to terminate the stream at that point.

7. Here we print out the name of the current Thread when each element is processed.

8. Finally, we use blockingSubscribe again just to print the output to standard out. In a real application, we would do something more interesting most likely.

The "readLineSupplier" method is defined as the following:

```
private static Supplier<String>
    readLineSupplier(BufferedReader reader) {
  return () -> { try {
    String line = reader.readLine();
    return line == null ? "EOF" : line;
  } catch (IOException ex)
    { throw new RuntimeException(ex); }};
}
```

The result of running this code for a given file would be each line of the file is printed out with "thread=RxCachedThreadScheduler-1" also printed out once for each line.

Backpressure

Hot Observables typically are candidates for using backpressure flow control strategies such as throttling, buffers, or windows. Beyond these options, you can convert an Observable into a Flowable with a backpressure strategy.

You can convert any Observable into a Flowable with backpressure support using the toFlowable(strategy) method. This would be done to mitigate any issues with the upstream (or publisher) emitting items faster than the downstream (or subscriber) can handle.

There are five main strategies to handle backpressure:

- *LATEST*: Only keep the latest item emitted, meaning you might miss some items if they are coming too fast.

- *DROP*: Drop newer items if they come too fast.

- *BUFFER*: Keep items in memory up to a certain point (usually you provide a limit).

- *ERROR*: Have the stream terminate with an error condition.

- *No strategy at all*: Without any strategy, the publisher would in effect be told to slow down (request(n) would not be called or would be called with a smaller number). This can only work in situations where this makes sense.

For example:

```
Observable.fromPublisher(pub) //1
.toFlowable(BackpressureStrategy.LATEST) //2
```

1. Create an Observable from some Publisher.

2. Convert the Observable into a Flowable with the strategy of LATEST (other available values are DROP, BUFFER, and ERROR).

Using `toFlowable(BackpressureStrategy.ERROR)` would cause an error to occur upon a backpressure event (more items being published than have been handled).

Likewise, the Flowable class has available the following methods to handle backpressure at any point in a flow:

- `onBackpressureLatest()`

- `onBackpressureDrop()`

- `onBackpressureBuffer()`

It also has several overloaded methods for providing configuration of the buffer such as capacity or an action to perform when capacity is reached.

See the RxJava <u>backpressure documentation</u> for more information on this topic.

Handling Errors

There are several ways to handle errors in RxJava streams:

- Handle errors without modifying the stream using "doOnError(Consumer<? super Throwable>)".

- Recover by returning a fixed value with onErrorReturnItem(T).

- Recover by returning a value based on the Exception with onErrorReturn(Function).

- Recover by returning a new Publisher with onErrorResumeNext(Publisher).

- Handle the error in the subscriber.

Testing

RxJava 2 includes built-in, test-friendly solutions such as TestSubscriber and TestObserver.

- *TestSubscriber*: A Subscriber that records events that you can make assertions upon

- *TestObserver*: An Observer that records events that you can make assertions upon

- *TestScheduler*: Can be used to have a strict control of test execution related to RxJava

TestSubscriber

For example, you can create a TestSubscriber by just calling "test()" on any Flowable:

```
TestSubscriber<Integer> ts =
  Flowable.range(1, 5).test();
assertEquals(5, ts.valueCount());
```

Calling "valueCount()" returns the total number of items emitted by the stream, five in this case.

TestSubscriber also has tons of other methods starting with "assert" such as assertError that can be used to assert certain things happen. For example:

```
Flowable<Integer> flowable = Flowable.create(source -> {
  source.onNext(1);
  source.onError(new RuntimeException());
}, BackpressureStrategy.LATEST);
TestSubscriber<Integer> ts = flowable.test();
ts.assertSubscribed();
ts.assertError(RuntimeException.class);
```

Here we call "assertError(Class)" with the type of Exception expected to be thrown by the Flowable. If it is not thrown, an AssertionError will be thrown, making the test fail.

TestObserver

Likewise, you can create a TestObserver by calling "test()" on any Observable:

```
TestObserver<Integer> ts =
Observable.range(1, 5).test();
assertEquals(5, ts.valueCount());
```

TestObserver and TestSubscriber both extend BaseTestConsumer and so have most of the same methods.

TestScheduler

TestScheduler can be used for testing time-related streams. For example:

```
TestScheduler scheduler = new TestScheduler(); //1
Observable<Long> tick = Observable
  .interval(1, TimeUnit.SECONDS, scheduler); //2
Observable<String> observable =
  Observable.just("foo", "bar", "biz", "baz") //3
  .zipWith(tick, (string, index) -> index + "-" + string);//4
TestObserver<String> testObserver = observable
  .subscribeOn(scheduler).test();//5
scheduler.advanceTimeBy(2300, TimeUnit.MILLISECONDS);//6
testObserver.assertNoErrors(); //7
testObserver.assertValues("0-foo", "1-bar");
testObserver.assertNotComplete();
```

1. Create the TestScheduler.

2. Create an interval Observable that will emit a number every second.

3. Create an Observable of just four strings.

4. Zip those two Observables together, combining them into one string, "index-string".

5. Make the Observable from step 4 subscribe on our TestScheduler and call "test()" to get an instance of TestObserver.

6. Manipulate the TestScheduler by calling "advanceTimeBy" with a value of 2.3 seconds so that two values should be emitted by the "tick" Observable.

7. Assert that there were no errors and the values we expect were emitted.

Using TestScheduler has the benefit of making RxJava streams behave as if a certain amount of time passed although it has not. This makes it so we can test RxJava logic that relies on any amount of time passing (hours or days) and our tests still run quickly. For example, the preceding test runs in less than one tenth of a second.

CHAPTER 5

Reactor

<u>Project Reactor</u> is Spring's implementation of Reactive Streams (in version 3 and beyond). It has two main publishers, Flux<T> and Mono<T>. It also uses Schedulers much like RxJava.

The Spring Framework has many integrations with Reactor that make it easier to use with other Spring projects, such as Spring Data and Spring Security.

Getting Started

If you have a Maven build, add the following to your pom file:

```
<dependency>
  <groupId>io.projectreactor</groupId>
  <artifactId>reactor-core</artifactId>
  <version>3.1.9.RELEASE</version>
</dependency>
<dependency>
  <groupId>io.projectreactor</groupId>
  <artifactId>reactor-test</artifactId>
  <version>3.1.9.RELEASE</version>
  <scope>test</scope>
</dependency>
```

© Adam L. Davis 2019
A. L. Davis, *Reactive Streams in Java*, https://doi.org/10.1007/978-1-4842-4176-9_5

For Gradle builds, add the following to your Gradle build file's dependencies:

```
compile 'io.projectreactor:reactor-core:3.1.9.RELEASE'
testCompile 'io.projectreactor:reactor-test:3.1.9.RELEASE'
```

Flux

Flux<T> is the main entry point for Reactor reactive streams and is similar to RxJava's Observable. Mono<T> is like a Flux but for zero to one element. Both Mono and Flux implement `org.reactivestreams.Publisher`.

```
import reactor.core.publisher.Flux;
import reactor.core.publisher.Mono;
```

Much like in RxJava, Reactor uses Schedulers to decide on what thread to run.

For example, you might create a range like the following and publish on "Schedulers.parallel()" which provides a thread cache for executing in parallel:

```
Flux.range(1, 100)
  .publishOn(Schedulers.parallel())
  .subscribe(v -> System.out.println(v));
```

The preceding code would print out the numbers 1 through 100.

Handling errors in Reactor is also very similar to RxJava. The following methods may be used on a Flux or Mono (generic types omitted for brevity):

- `onErrorResume(Function)`: Takes the exception and returns a different Publisher as a fallback or secondary stream.

- onErrorMap(Function): Takes the exception and allows you to modify it or return a completely new Exception if you prefer.

- onErrorReturn(T): Provides a default value to use when an error arises.

- doOnError(Consumer<? super Throwable>): Allows you to handle the error without effecting the underlying stream in any way.

Errors are always ending events for a Flux or Mono and should be handled by the Subscriber. However, many times, such as in the preceding example, an error is not possible and therefore does not need to be handled.

Mono

Mono is much like a Flux but for just one or zero elements. Think of it like a translation of Java 8's Optional class into the Reactive Streams world. For example, the following would print out the value "hello":

```
Mono.just("hello").subscribe(v -> System.out.println(v));
```

Mono is very similar to Flux except that it has methods like

- justOrEmpty(T): Takes a nullable value and converts into a Mono. If null, the result is the same as Mono. empty().

- justOrEmpty(Optional): Takes an Optional and converts into a Mono directly.

Unlike Java's Optional, Mono can handle errors, among other things. For example, a method that returns Mono might do the following:

```
return Mono.error(new RuntimeException("your error"))
```

The corresponding code can handle errors from a Mono in the same way as with a Flux (using onErrorResume, onErrorMap, or onErrorReturn).

Creating a Flux or Mono

You can create a Flux from fixed data (cold) or programmatically from dynamic data (hot).

The following are some different ways to create a cold Flux:

```
Flux<String> flux1 = Flux.just("a", "b", "foobar"); //1
List<String> iterable = Arrays.asList("a", "b", "foobar");
Flux<String> flux2 = Flux.fromIterable(iterable); //2
Flux<Integer> numbers = Flux.range(1, 64); //3
```

1. Create a Flux from a list of values.

2. Create a Flux from an Iterable.

3. Create a range from 1 to 64.

Here's how to create a simple Mono:

```
Mono<String> noData = Mono.empty(); //1
Mono<String> data = Mono.just("foo"); //2
```

4. Create an empty Mono.

5. Create a Mono with one element.

You can programmatically create a hot or cold Flux using one of the generate, create, or push methods. If the data is of a continuous nature, such as user input, a WebSocket, or network packets, it would be considered hot.

The generate method (in one variety) takes a Supplier and a BiFunction. The function takes as parameters the current state and a SynchronousSink<T> which can be used to publish the next state of the stream. For example, the following uses an `AtomicLong` instance to increment the numbers 0 through 10 and supplies the square of each number:

```
Flux<Long> squares = Flux.generate(
  AtomicLong::new, //1
  (state, sink) -> {
    long i = state.getAndIncrement();
    sink.next(i * i); //2
    if (i == 10) sink.complete(); //3
    return state;
});
```

1. The constructor of AtomicLong is used as the supplier.

2. After incrementing, supply the square of the number to the sink.

3. When the number is 10, the complete() method is called, which calls `onComplete` to any subscriber, closing out the Flux.

The create method takes a Consumer<? super FluxSink<T>> that exposes a FluxSink<T> instance with next, error, and complete methods. This allows you to arbitrarily publish data onto a Flux in any way you see fit.

The preceding code would produce a Flux of the squares of the numbers from zero to ten.

For example, the following demonstrates registering a `MessageListener` which handles a list of messages:

```
Flux<String> bridge = Flux.create(sink -> {
 messageProcessor.register(
  new MessageListener<String>() {
  public void handle(List<String> chunks) {
```

```
  for(String s : chunks) {
   sink.next(s);
  }
 }
 public void processComplete() {
  sink.complete();
 }
 public void processError(Throwable e) {
  sink.error(e);
 }
});
});
```

Here sink's type is FluxSink<String>. If the messages processed in the preceding code have a single-threaded source, the push method can be used instead of create. The push method has the same type signature as create, and so it is used in a similar way. FluxSink's methods return FluxSink, allowing for method chaining, so the following example is possible:

```
Flux.push((FluxSink sink) -> {
   sink.next(1).next(2).next(3).complete();
}).subscribe(System.out::println);
```

This would print out just the values 1, 2, and 3.

Schedulers

The Schedulers class under the reactor.core.scheduler package provides many static methods for Schedulers that determine what Thread or Threads your code will run on.

The following are some of those static methods and what they mean:

- `Schedulers.immediate()`: The current thread.

- `Schedulers.single()`: A single, reusable thread. Note that this method reuses the same thread for all callers, until the Scheduler is disposed. If you want a per-call dedicated thread, use `Schedulers.newSingle()` for each call.

- `Schedulers.newSingle()`: Creates a new Thread each time it is called to be used by the underlying Flux.

- `Schedulers.elastic()`: An elastic thread pool. It creates new worker pools as needed and reuses idle ones. Worker pools that stay idle for too long (default is 60 seconds) are disposed. This is a good choice for I/O blocking work for instance. `Schedulers.elastic()` is a handy way to give a blocking process its own thread, so that it does not tie up other resources.

- `Schedulers.parallel()`: A fixed pool of workers. It creates as many workers as you have CPU cores.

- `Schedulers.fromExecutor(Executor)`: Creates a Scheduler to use the given Executor, allowing you to use your extensive knowledge of Java's Executors.

For example, let's take our example of generating squares and make it run in parallel:

```
List<Integer> squares = new ArrayList<>();
Flux.range(1, 64).flatMap(v -> // 1
Mono.just(v)
 .subscribeOn(Schedulers.newSingle("comp"))
 .map(w -> w * w)) //2
```

```
.doOnError(ex -> ex.printStackTrace()) // 3
.doOnComplete(() -> System.out.println("Completed")) // 4
.subscribeOn(Schedulers.immediate())
.subscribe(squares::add); //5
```

1. First we use `Flux.range` to take the range from 1 to 64 and call `flatMap` (which takes a lambda expression that converts each value in the range into a new Reactor type, Mono in this case).

2. Using `Schedulers.newSingle(name)`, we create a new single thread for each value, and passing to `subscribeOn` will cause the mapping expression to be executed on that single thread. Keep in mind we are describing the execution of the Mono here, not the initial Flux.

3. We provide exception handling code using `doOnError` just in case.

4. Using `doOnComplete` we print out "Completed" when the whole execution is finished.

5. Finally, we subscribe to the Flux (without this step, nothing would ever happen) and add the result to our list of squares.

The result of running this code will be that the squares List has the value of every square from 1 to 64.

Here we see once again how in Reactive Streams everything can become a stream, even a single value. By creating a Mono for each value in the range, we're able to use Reactor to declare what kind of threading we want for every calculation. In this case, since we are using `newSingle`, all of the processing will be done in parallel with a new thread for all 64 values.

However, this is probably not the most efficient implementation since creating lots of Threads causes a lot of overhead. Instead, we should use Schedulers.parallel() so that the exact number of Threads your CPU can handle will be created. In this way, Reactor takes care of the details for you.

Pull Events

If you have more of a "pull" situation (events are created by polling a source), you can use the Flux.create(FluxSink) method. For example, the following code creates a Flux that polls a channel (some imaginary class representing a stream of Strings from outside of Reactor) for new events:

```
Flux<String> bridge = Flux.create(sink -> {
sink.onRequest(n -> channel.poll(n)) //1
  .onCancel(channel::cancel) // 2
  .onDispose(channel::close); // 3
  channel.register(sink::next); //4
});
```

1. Poll for events from the channel when requests are made with the given number. This "n" is the number of items requested.

2. Call the channel's cancel method when the Flux is cancelled.

3. The channel.close method is given to onDispose to be invoked for complete, error, or cancel.

4. Finally, register the sink's "next" method as a listener to the channel.

Keep in mind that the Consumer passed to onRequest will not be called multiple times for no reason. It will be called with some number (e.g., 256) and then not called again until a significant number of items have been published to the Flux (i.e., sink.next called many times).

Reminder   The code examples used in this book are available on
GitHub.

Handling Backpressure

Reactor, like all implementations of Reactive Streams, has the ability to
handle backpressure. Simply use one of the following methods on a Flux (or
others not listed) to specify which backpressure strategy you want to use:

- *onBackpressureBuffer()*: Buffers all items until they can
  be handled downstream.

- *onBackpressureBuffer(maxSize)*: Buffers items up to the
  given count.

- *onBackpressureBuffer(maxSize, BufferOverflowStrategy)*:
  Buffers items up to the given count and allows you to
  specify the strategy to use when and if the buffer is full.
  BufferOverflowStrategy is an enum that has three values:
  DROP_OLDEST, which drops the oldest items in the
  buffer, DROP_LATEST which drops the newer items, and
  ERROR which would terminate the stream with an error.

- *onBackpressureLatest()*: Similar to keeping a buffer of
  only the last item added. If the downstream does not
  keep up with upstream, only the latest element will be
  given downstream.

- *onBackpressureError()*: Ends the Flux with an error
  (calling the downstream Subscriber's onError)
  with an IllegalStateException from Exceptions.
  failWithOverflow() if more items were produced
  upstream than requested downstream.

- *onBackpressureDrop()*: Drops any items produced above what was requested. This would be useful, for example, in UI code to drop user input that can't be handled immediately.

- *onBackpressureDrop(Consumer)*: Drops any items produced above what was requested and calls the given Consumer for each dropped item.

With each of these methods, the strategy only applies when items are produced on the stream faster than they can be handled. If that's not the case, for example, with a cold stream, no backpressure strategy is necessary.

For example, we might want to take a Flux named "bridge" created earlier that is a stream of user input and buffer up to 256 items like the following:

```
bridge.onBackpressureBuffer(256)
```

Also keep in mind that Reactor is not magic, and some care should be taken when considering backpressure strategies.

Reactor has excellent online <u>documentation</u> for consideration.

Context

Since version 3.1.0, Reactor comes with an advanced feature that is somewhat comparable to ThreadLocal but applied to a Flux or a Mono instead of a Thread: the Context.

Reactor's Context is much like an immutable Map or key/value store. It is stored transparently from the Subscriber upward through the Subscription. Context is Reactor specific and does not work with the other Reactive Streams implementations.

When setting up the Context, you should not define it toward the beginning of the Flux. This is because it starts at the subscriber and is passed upstream. For example, do not do this:

```
// this is WRONG!
Flux<Integer> flux =
  Flux.just(1).subscriberContext(Context.of("pid", 123));
```

Instead you should define it toward the end since it propagates "backward" up the chain. For example:

```
Flux<Integer> flux = Flux.just(1); //1
Flux<String> stringFlux = flux.flatMap(i ->
  Mono.subscriberContext().map(ctx -> i + " pid: " +
    ctx.getOrDefault("pid", 0))); //2
// supply context here:
StepVerifier.create( //3
  stringFlux.subscriberContext(Context.of("pid", 123)))
    .expectNext("1 pid: 123") //4
    .verifyComplete();
```

1. Create a Flux of just one value.

2. Use flatMap, access the Context, and use it to create a String value using the "pid" key. We use the static method on Mono, subscriberContext() to access the value from the Context by calling "getOrDefault" on it.

3. This uses the **StepVerifier** (which we cover next) to verify that we get the expected value. The StepVerifier subscribes to the Flux after setting the Context using the "subscriberContext" method.

4. Call "expectNext" with a value of "1 pid: 123" which is what we expect from setting the value 123 with the key of "pid" on the Context.

Context is useful for storing data that is peripheral to the Flux, but still important. For example, sometimes we have some identifier that represents the action or the user that initiated an action, and we want to include it in log outputs (like what <u>MDC</u> is used for in logback).

Testing

Automated testing is always a good idea, and it would be nice to have tools to directly test Reactive Streams. Luckily, Reactor comes with a few elements dedicated to testing which are gathered into their own artifact we included earlier: reactor-test.

The two main uses of reactor-test are the following:

- Testing that a sequence follows a given scenario with StepVerifier

- Producing data in order to test the behavior of operators (including your own operators) downstream with TestPublisher

StepVerifier

Reactor's StepVerifier can be used to verify the behavior of a Reactor Publisher (Flux or Mono). StepVerifier is an interface used for testing that can be created using one of several static methods on StepVerifier itself.

Here's a simple example of a JUnit test utilizing StepVerifier:

```
@Test
public void testStepVerifier_Mono_error() {
  Mono<String> monoError = Mono.error(
new RuntimeException("error")); //1
  StepVerifier.create(monoError) //2
```

```
    .expectErrorMessage("error") //3
    .verify(); //4
}
```

1. Create a Mono wrapping a RuntimeException imitating an actual error state.

2. Create a StepVerifier wrapping that Mono.

3. Declare that an onError event is expected and the Exception's error message is "error".

4. Must call verify() at the end. This will throw an AssertionError if any expectations are not met.

We can also create a Mono of just one string and verify it, for example:

```
@Test public void testStepVerifier_Mono_foo() {
Mono<String> foo = Mono.just("foo"); //1
StepVerifier.create(foo) //2
  .expectNext("foo") //3
  .verifyComplete(); //4
}
```

1. Create a Mono wrapping one value, "foo".

2. Create a StepVerifier wrapping that Mono.

3. Expect onNext is called with "foo".

4. Call verifyComplete() has the same effect as verify() but also expects onComplete was called.

Here we will test a Flux with three values and timeout if it takes too long:

```
@Test public void testStepVerifier_Flux() {
Flux<Integer> flux = Flux.just(1, 4, 9); //1
StepVerifier.create(flux) //2
```

```
.expectNext(1) //3
.expectNext(4)
.expectNext(9)
.expectComplete() //4
.verify(Duration.ofSeconds(10)); //5
}
```

1. Create a Flux of just three numbers.

2. Create a StepVerifier wrapping that Flux.

3. Call expectNext for each value expected.

4. Call expectComplete to expect onComplete to be called.

5. Finally, you must call verify() at the end. This variation of verify takes a Duration timeout value. Here it is 10 seconds. This can be useful to prevent the Test from hanging in cases where a Publisher might never call onComplete.

TestPublisher

The TestPublisher<T> class offers the ability to provide finely tuned data for test purposes. TestPublisher is a Reactive Streams Publisher<T> but can be converted to either a Flux or Mono using flux() or mono() methods.

TestPublisher has the following methods:

- *next(T) and next(T, T...)*: Triggers 1–n onNext signals.

- *emit(T...)*: Does the same as next and also terminates with an onComplete signal.

- *complete()*: Terminates with an onComplete signal.

- *error(Throwable)*: Terminates with an onError signal.

The following demonstrates how you might use TestPublisher:

```
TestPublisher<Object> publisher = TestPublisher.create(); //1
Flux<Object> stringFlux = publisher.flux(); //2
List list = new ArrayList(); //3
stringFlux.subscribe(next -> list.add(next), ex ->
  ex.printStackTrace()); //4
publisher.emit("foo", "bar"); //5
assertEquals(2, list.size()); //6
assertEquals("foo", list.get(0));
assertEquals("bar", list.get(1));
```

1. Create the TestPublisher instance.

2. Convert it to a Flux.

3. Create a new List. For test purposes we will use this list to collect values from the publisher.

4. Subscribe to the publisher using two lambda expressions for onNext and onError. This will add each value emitted from the publisher to the list.

5. Emit the values "foo" and "bar" from the TestPublisher.

6. Assert that two values were added to the list and they are what we expect.

Note that you must subscribe to the TestPublisher before emitting any values.

CHAPTER 6

Akka Streams

<u>Akka Streams</u> implements the Reactive Streams standard within the larger Akka concurrency project.

Akka Streams is built on the philosophy of providing a minimal and consistent Application programming interface (API) that is extremely compositional, meaning it is broken into pieces that can be combined in many ways.

Unlike RxJava and Reactor, the topology of streams (flows) in Akka Streams is immutable once they have been materialized. This means that you must be explicit to convert a flow into a Reactive Streams interface to have a dynamic topology (as we'll cover later on).

Although most familiar in Scala-based applications, Akka Streams has a Java-specific API, and the documentation lets you select Java or Scala as your target language with specific examples for each.

Akka Streams uses the concepts of Source and Sink to correspond roughly with Publisher and Subscriber of other Reactive Streams frameworks. It also has the concept of Flow which is roughly equivalent to Processor and Graphs which are like blueprints of Flows, Sinks, or Sources.

© Adam L. Davis 2019
A. L. Davis, *Reactive Streams in Java*, https://doi.org/10.1007/978-1-4842-4176-9_6

Getting Started

If you have a <u>Maven</u> build, add the following to your pom file:

```
<dependency>
        <groupId>com.typesafe.akka</groupId>
        <artifactId>akka-stream_2.12</artifactId>
        <version>2.5.16</version>
</dependency>
<dependency>
        <groupId>com.typesafe.akka</groupId>
        <artifactId>akka-stream-testkit_2.12</artifactId>
        <version>2.5.16</version>
        <scope>test</scope>
</dependency>
```

For <u>Gradle</u> builds, add the following to your Gradle build file's dependencies:

```
compile 'com.typesafe.akka:akka-stream_2.12:2.5.16'
testCompile 'com.typesafe.akka:akka-stream-testkit_2.12:2.5.16'
```

Use the following imports:

```
import akka.stream.*;
import akka.stream.javadsl.*;
```

In this example we will be taking a stream of messages and extracting all messages that begin with Error:

```
final ActorSystem system = ActorSystem.create(
"reactive-messages"); //1
final Materializer mat = ActorMaterializer.create(system); //2
Source<String, NotUsed> messages = Source
.single("Error: test message");
```

```
final Source<String, NotUsed> errors =
        messages.filter(m -> m.startsWith("Error")) //3
        .map(m -> m.toString()); //4
errors.runWith(Sink.foreach(System.out::println), mat); //5
```

1. We create the Akka ActorSystem to define the multithreaded environment for execution. We provide a name "reactive-messages" which is optional and gives a logical name to the ActorSystem.

2. The execution environment (similar to Schedulers in RxJava) is known as a Materializer here. Unlike RxJava, the developer controls concurrency by calling methods like async() and mapAsync(int,Function) on a Source or Flow.

3. We filter out only the error messages.

4. Although not necessary, we call toString on each message to illustrate using the map method.

5. Finally, we use runWith and pass in a Sink which prints out each error message.

Although here we are using the foreach Sink, any sink could be used, including user-defined sinks.

To avoid conceptual conflicts with the existing flatMap in Scala, Akka Streams uses flatMapConcat, flatMapMerge, and mapConcat. The mapConcat method expects Iterables returned from the function, not streams. The other two methods act as their names suggest, either merging streams or appending them sequentially.

ActorMaterializer

The ActorMaterializer in Akka Streams is similar to Schedulers in the other two Reactive Streams implementations but not the same. Unlike Schedulers, there are not several predefined singletons to choose from; instead you should generally create one for your whole application and specify some general settings.

An ActorMaterializer is created in the following way:

```
public static Materializer createMaterializer() {
 final ActorSystem system = ActorSystem.create(); // 1
 ActorMaterializerSettings settings =
  ActorMaterializerSettings.create(system) //2
        .withMaxFixedBufferSize(100) //3
        .withInputBuffer(8, 16); //4
 return ActorMaterializer.create(settings,system);//5
```

1. Create the ActorSystem.

2. Optionally create ActorMaterializerSettings. This allows you to configure internal settings used by Akka Streams to enhance performance for your particular project.

3. Set maximum fixed buffer size to 100. Stream elements which have explicit buffers (like mapAsync, mapAsyncUnordered, flatMapMerge, Source.actorRef, Source.queue, etc.) that request a lower buffer size will use this value as the initial fixed buffer size. The default is very large to make failures happen earlier, not when scaling up. You might change it if you want to use a small amount of memory, for example.

4. Set the initial and maximum size of internal stream buffers. Here we set the initial value to 8 and maximum to 16, which are the defaults.

5. Finally create the ActorMaterializer with the given settings and ActorSystem.

Sinks, Flows, and Graphs

One of the interesting things about Akka Streams is that every part can be defined, is immutable, and can be reused independently. For this purpose, Akka Streams has the concept of Flow, Graph, Source, and Sink.

- *Flow*: A Flow has both an input and an output. So, you can define a Flow with only the type of the data that will be streamed, without the actual data. It is similar to org. reactivestreams.Processor which is both a Publisher and a Subscriber.

- *Graph*: A Graph can define any arbitrary branching and recombining of streams. A Graph is immutable, thread-safe, and reusable. A Graph that is self-contained (has no input or output) is a RunnableGraph and can be materialized.

- *Source*: A Source has exactly one output. It is a source of data, similar to a Publisher, and can be created in many different ways.

- *Sink*: As seen before, a Sink is the ending point of a stream. It represents what we do with the data. It has exactly one input.

Using Flow, you can define a Sink separately from defining any sources. For example, this sink would save to a file:

```
public Sink<String, CompletionStage<IOResult>> lineSink(
        String filename) {
  return Flow.of(String.class)
    .map(s -> ByteString.fromString(s.toString() + "\n"))
    .toMat(FileIO.toPath(Paths.get(filename)),
        Keep.right());
}
```

First, we create a Flow of type "String"; this declares what type you are expecting. Second, we map each string into a ByteString. At this point, the type is now Flow<ByteString>. Lastly, we call toMat (which is short for toMaterialized) to write the result to a file using an existing Sink (FileIO is part of the Akka Streams Java DSL). We specify Keep.right() to keep the auxiliary information from toPath.

The Sink, once defined, can be used multiple times. Notice that defining the Sink does not complete any action. No save has taken place yet until we materialize it with some Source. For example:

```
public void saveTextFile(List<String> text) {
        Sink<String, CompletionStage<IOResult>> sink =
                lineSink("testfile.txt");
        Source.from(text).runWith(sink, materializer);
}
```

This method would take a List of Strings, create a Source from them, and then save them to a file using the Sink from the lineSink method.

Graphs can be created using the GraphDSL. For example, using the previously defined methods, we can create a Graph of a SinkShape like so:

```java
public Graph<SinkShape<String>, NotUsed> createFileSinkGraph()
{
    return GraphDSL.create(builder -> {
    FlowShape<String, String> flowShape = builder
     .add(Flow.of(String.class).async()); //1
    var sink = lineSink("testfile.txt"); //2
    var sinkShape = builder.add(sink); //3

    builder.from(flowShape.out()).to(sinkShape); //4
    return new SinkShape<>(flowShape.in()); //5
  });
}
```

1.   Call builder.add with a Flow to get a FlowShape. Here we create an asynchronous Flow.

2.   Create a new Sink<String> by calling our lineSink method.

3.   Create a SinkShape<String> from that sink.

4.   Link the output from the flowShape to the sinkShape.

5.   Return a new SinkShape using the input from the flowShape. We have now created the Graph of a SinkShape that will save text lines to a file.

We can use this graph by calling Sink.fromGraph to create a Sink:

```java
public void saveTextFileUsingGraph(List<String> text) {
  Sink.fromGraph(createFileSinkGraph())
    .runWith(Source.from(text), materializer);
}
```

The preceding code would use the Graph we created to create a new Sink and run it with a Source created from the given List, thus saving the text, one line per element of the list.

Backpressure

Backpressure strategies can be defined on the stream to describe what to do when too many elements are produced. For example, we can buffer our messages stream:

```
messages
        .buffer(100, OverflowStrategy.dropHead())
```

This would buffer 100 elements, dropping the oldest (dropHead). You should pick whatever strategy best fits your problem space.

Other options include

- *dropTail()*: Drops the newest elements from the buffer.

- *dropBuffer()*: An aggressive strategy that drops the entire buffer once it is full.

- *dropNew()*: Drops any new elements when the buffer is full.

- *backpressure()*: The strategy would cause backpressure signal to be pushed upstream if the buffer is full. In other words, the amount requested from upstream would fall to zero until the buffer was no longer full.

- *fail()*: Fails the stream entirely when the buffer is full.

Interoperation with Reactive Streams API

Due to Akka Streams' immutable topology requirements, it can be surprising to people familiar with other Reactive Streams libraries.

In order to obtain a Publisher or Subscriber from an Akka Stream topology, a corresponding Sink.asPublisher or Source.asSubscriber element must be used.

A Sink must be created with Sink.asPublisher(AsPublisher.WITH_FANOUT) (for enabling fan-out support) where broadcast behavior is needed for interoperation with other Reactive Streams implementations. If "AsPublisher.WITHOUT_FANOUT" is used instead, the resulting Publisher will only allow one Subscriber.

An Akka Streams Flow can also be converted to a Processor using Flow's toProcessor() method; however, it is also limited to only one Subscriber.

To get around these limitations, and create dynamic stream handling within Akka Streams, you can use MergeHub, BroadcastHub, and PartitionHub.

MergeHub, BroadcastHub, and PartitionHub

For dynamically defined flows of data that need to have multiple consumers or multiple producers of data, Akka Streams has the following classes:

- A MergeHub allows any number of flows to go into a single Sink.

- A BroadcastHub can be used to consume elements from a common producer by a dynamic set of consumers.

- A PartitionHub can be used to route elements from a common producer to a dynamic set of consumers. The selection of consumer is done with a function and each element can only be routed to one consumer.

For example, here is a simple use case of a MergeHub:

```
Sink<String, CompletionStage<Done>> consumer =
        Sink.foreach(System.out::println); //1
int bufferSize = 8;
RunnableGraph<Sink<String, NotUsed>> runnableGraph =
    MergeHub.of(String.class, bufferSize)
        .to(consumer); //2
Sink<String, NotUsed> toConsumer =
    runnableGraph.run(materializer); //3
```

1. A simple consumer that will print to the console.

2. Attach a MergeHub Source to the consumer. This will materialize to a corresponding Sink when run. The buffer size is used per producer.

3. Finally we must run and materialize the runnableGraph to get the Sink. This Sink can be materialized any number of times, and every element that enters it will be consumed by the "consumer" defined in step 1.

For more information about MergeHub, BroadcastHub, and PartitionHub, see the documentation.

Testing

Akka Streams includes a testkit to assist in creating tests around your application. It includes the following:

- *TestKit*: Has a method that is useful for shutting down the ActorSystem between each test

- *TestSink*: Enables probing of an Akka Stream Source directly using a TestSubscriber.Probe<T> instance

- *TestSource*: Enables probing of a Sink using a
  TestPublisher.Probe<String> probe instance

Add the following imports to the test class:

```
import static org.junit.Assert.*;
import static org.hamcrest.CoreMatchers.*;
import akka.NotUsed;
import akka.actor.ActorSystem;
import akka.japi.Pair;
import akka.stream.ActorMaterializer;
import akka.stream.javadsl.*;
import akka.stream.testkit.*;
import akka.stream.testkit.javadsl.TestSink;
import akka.testkit.javadsl.TestKit;
import org.junit.*;
```

Define our setup and tearDown methods:

```
ActorSystem system;
ActorMaterializer materializer;
@Before
public void setup() {
  system = ActorSystem.create();
  materializer = ActorMaterializer.create(system);
}
@After
public void tearDown() {
  TestKit.shutdownActorSystem(system);
}
```

Now we can write tests using TestSink to probe any Source. For example:

```
@Test
public void test_a_source() {
  Sink<Object, TestSubscriber.Probe<Object>> sink =
        TestSink.probe(system); //1
  Source<Object, NotUsed> sourceUnderTest =
        Source.single("test"); //2
  sourceUnderTest.runWith(sink, materializer) //3
        .request(1)
        .expectNext("test")
        .expectComplete();
}
```

1. Create the TestSink instance.

2. Create the Source we want to test. In a real test, this would come from some part of your production code.

3. Run the Source with the TestSink and use the resulting TestSubscriber.Probe<T> instance to request one value and expect it to be "test". Calling expectComplete() means we expect the Source to send the "on-complete" signal, and if not it will through an AssertionError.

We can also test Sinks using the TestSource.probe(ActorSystem) method as follows:

```
Sink<String, CompletionStage<List<String>>>
        sinkUnderTest = Sink.seq(); //1
final Pair<TestPublisher.Probe<String>,
 CompletionStage<List<String>>> stagePair =
   TestSource.<String>probe(system)
        .toMat(sinkUnderTest, Keep.both()) //2
        .run(materializer);
final TestPublisher.Probe<String> probe =
        stagePair.first(); //3
final CompletionStage<List<String>> future =
        stagePair.second();
probe.expectRequest(); //4
probe.sendNext("test");
probe.sendError(new Exception("boom!"));
try {
  future.toCompletableFuture().get(2, TimeUnit.SECONDS); //5
  assert false;
} catch (ExecutionException ee) {
  final Throwable exception = ee.getCause();
  assertEquals(exception.getMessage(), "boom!"); //6
}
```

1. Get an instance of the Sink we want to test.

2. Create and materialize the TestSource with sinkUnderTest and keep both the materialized value and auxiliary value using Keep.both().

3. Get references to both the TestPublisher.
    Probe<String> and the CompletionStage (future) as
    we will use them later.

4. Call several methods on the probe to expect the Sink
    requested data, send some data, then call sendError
    on the probe with an Exception instance.

5. Convert the CompletionStage from the previous
    step to a CompletableFuture and call "get" with a
    timeout of two seconds (just in case the underlying
    future would never complete).

6. Finally, assert that the Exception was thrown and it
    has the message "boom!"

CHAPTER 7

Android and RxJava

RxAndroid, RxBinding, and RxLifecycle provide RxJava bindings for Android. This makes using RxJava in an Android application much easier.

Since the release of Android Studio 2.4, it has supported using Java 8's lambda syntax which we can make heavy use of in our RxJava-related code.

RxBinding is an open source library of Java binding APIs for Android UI widgets from the platform and support libraries.
For this chapter we'll build a simple example application with RxAndroid, RxBinding, RxLifecycle, and RxJava using Android Studio. The code is available on GitHub.

Getting Started

If you have not already, go download the latest Android Studio for your operating system and install and run it. Once Android Studio has started, perform the following steps to get started:

1. Create a new project by selecting File ➤ New Project from the menu and give it a name (such as RxAndroidTest).

© Adam L. Davis 2019
A. L. Davis, *Reactive Streams in Java*, https://doi.org/10.1007/978-1-4842-4176-9_7

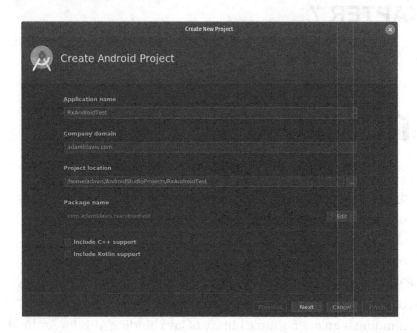

2.   Select 8.0 (Oreo) as the target version.

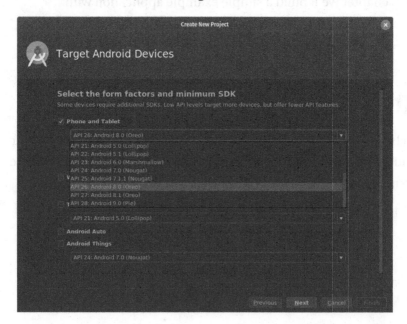

3. When prompted, select "Login Activity" when it says "Add an Activity to Mobile".

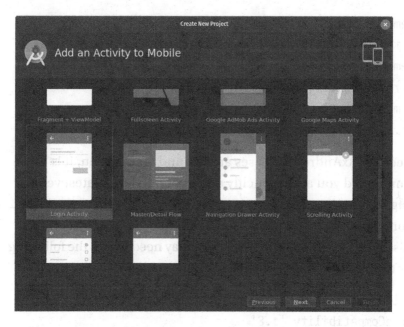

4. Then, click the module name on the left-hand side (such as "app"), press F4, and then make sure your Java version is set to at least 8 (allow lambdas).

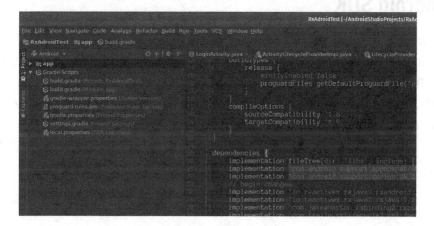

After your project is started, add the required dependencies to your build file (app/build.gradle):

```
implementation
 'io.reactivex.rxjava2:rxandroid:2.1.0'
implementation
 'io.reactivex.rxjava2:rxjava:2.2.2'
implementation
 'com.jakewharton.rxbinding2:rxbinding:2.1.1'
```

Because RxAndroid releases are few and far between, it is recommended you also explicitly depend on RxJava's latest version for bug fixes and new features (see the RxJava GitHub for the latest 2.x version).

Also, to enable Java 8 code style, you may need to add the following under the "android" block of build.gradle:

```
compileOptions {
 sourceCompatibility '1.8'
 targetCompatibility '1.8'
}
```

Android SDK

Before your project can be compiled, you need to have one or more versions of Android Software Development Kit (SDK) installed.

To do this, choose the "File" menu then "Settings..." and then type in "SDK" in the search box and select "Android SDK". Make sure to install at least one Android SDK and accept the license.

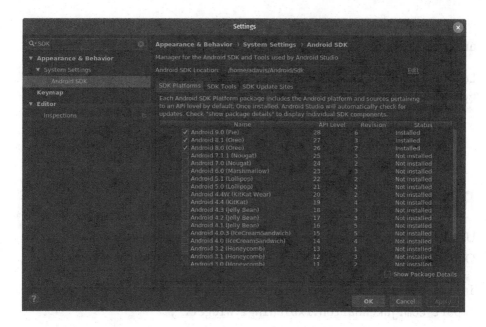

Android Schedulers

RxAndroid provides AndroidSchedulers which enables you to run on Android-specific threads such as the main thread. For example:

```
Observable.just("one", "two", "three", "four")
 .observeOn(AndroidSchedulers.mainThread())
 .subscribe(each ->
        System.out.println(each.toUpperCase()));
```

This would run the actions of this Observable on Android's main thread. This is useful since updates to the UI should occur on the main thread.

To find out what thread your code is executing on, just use Thread. currentThread().getName(). For example, we could replace the last line in the preceding code with the following to print out the name of the current thread:

```
System.out.println(
        Thread.currentThread().getName())
```

You can also use AndroidSchedulers to create a Scheduler around any arbitrary Looper. For example:

```
Looper looper = Looper.myLooper();
RxView.clicks(button)
  .observeOn(AndroidSchedulers.from(looper))
  .subscribe();
```

RxBinding

Using RxBinding, you can easily turn Android UI events into RxJava Observables. To start, add the following imports to LoginActivity.java:

```
import com.jakewharton.rxbinding2.view.*;
import com.jakewharton.rxbinding2.widget.*;
import io.reactivex.Observable;
```

For example, let's take a button and subscribe to click events. Open "LoginActivity.java" and find the line that starts with "Button mEmailSignInButton".

Find and comment out the following code:

```
Button mEmailSignInButton = (Button)
        findViewById(R.id.email_sign_in_button);
mEmailSignInButton.setOnClickListener(
        new OnClickListener() {
        @Override
        public void onClick(View view) {
          attemptLogin();
        }
});
```

This can be replaced using RxAndroid with the following:

```
Button button = (Button)
findViewById(R.id.email_sign_in_button);
RxView.clicks(button).subscribe(event -> {
        attemptLogin();
});
```

We can also observe text changes on an EditText, for example:

```
RxTextView.textChangeEvents(editText)
        .subscribe(e -> log(e.text().toString()));
```

Using these bindings, we can combine the Observables together in different ways to achieve our final goal. For example, add the following code:

```
Observable<TextViewTextChangeEvent>
        emailChangeObservable =
        RxTextView.textChangeEvents(mEmailView);
Observable<TextViewTextChangeEvent>
        passwordChangeObservable =
        RxTextView.textChangeEvents(mPasswordView);
// force-disable the button
button.setEnabled(false);
Disposable d = Observable.combineLatest(
        emailChangeObservable, passwordChangeObservable,
        (emailObservable, passwordObservable) -> {
        boolean emailCheck =
        emailObservable.text().length() >= 3;
        boolean passwordCheck =
        passwordObservable.text().length() >= 3;
        return emailCheck && passwordCheck;
}).subscribe(
        enabled -> button.setEnabled(enabled));
```

In this example, the submit button will only be clickable if both forms have more than three characters each.

The Disposable instance above (d) holds a reference to the view, so we must unsubscribe from the stream or cause it to terminate to prevent memory leaks. This can be achieved in a consistent way using the RxLifecycle library.

RxLifecycle

RxLifecycle is an open source library for binding to lifecycle events of Android components. This can be useful for dropping subscriptions and avoiding memory leaks on destroy/pause events for example.

To get started with RxLifecycle, add the following dependencies to your "build.gradle" file:

```
implementation 'com.trello.rxlifecycle2:rxlifecycle:2.2.2'
implementation
'com.trello.rxlifecycle2:rxlifecycle-android:2.2.2'
implementation
'com.trello.rxlifecycle2:rxlifecycle-components:2.2.2'
```

Next, add the following imports to your Activity:

```
import com.trello.rxlifecycle2.components.support\
       .RxAppCompatActivity;
```

Then change the LoginActivity to extend the "Rx" equivalent (RxAppCompatActivity in this case):

```
public class LoginActivity extends RxAppCompatActivity
implements LoaderCallbacks<Cursor> {
```

Finally, you can now use "compose" and RxLifecycle to bind a sequence to the lifecycle events. For example:

```
@Override
public void onResume() {
super.onResume();
Observable<Long> mySequence = Observable.interval
(200, TimeUnit.MILLISECONDS);
mySequence
 .doOnNext(x -> System.out.println(
        "poll the server"))
 .observeOn(AndroidSchedulers.mainThread())
 .compose(bindToLifecycle())
 .subscribe();
}
```

Here "mySequence" could be any RxJava type such as Observable, Flowable, Single, or Maybe. In this case, "Observable.interval" will emit a value every 200 milliseconds.

RxLifecycle determines the appropriate time to end the sequence, for example: if subscribing during START, it will terminate on STOP; if you subscribe after PAUSE, it will terminate at the next destruction event.

RxLifecycle will then terminate the sequence when appropriate with the following consequences depending on the type of the original sequence:

- *Observable, Flowable, and Maybe*: Emits onCompleted()

- *Single and Completable*: Emits onError(Cancellation Exception)

In the preceding example, by putting the code in "onResume", this would cause our polling to take place after resume and stop upon a pause event.

Putting It Together

Let's use RxLifecycle and RxAndroid to improve our code from earlier:

```
Observable.combineLatest(
        emailChangeObservable,
        passwordChangeObservable,
        (emailObservable, passwordObservable) -> {
        boolean emailCheck =
        emailObservable.text().length() >= 3;
        boolean passwordCheck =
        passwordObservable.text().length() >= 3;
        return emailCheck && passwordCheck; //1
})
.compose(bindToLifecycle()) //2
.observeOn(AndroidSchedulers.mainThread()) //3
.subscribe(
        enabled -> button.setEnabled(enabled)); //4
```

1. We have the same "combineLatest" as before to ensure both inputs have at least three characters.

2. We use our RxActivity instance to bind to the lifecycle so that our Observable will stop when appropriate.

3. We observe on the Android main thread.

4. Finally, we subscribe to do what we want with the stream, which is enable or disable to the "login" button in this case.

Since we called "bindToLifecycle" within the "onCreate" method, RxLifecycle will cause the sequence to terminate on the "opposite" action, "onDestroy" in this case. This will release our reference to the email and password view, preventing memory leaks.

Using RxJava

Using basic RxJava operations, we can improve "noisy" data inputs to prevent things like accidental double-clicks causing an action to occur twice.

Using the "debounce" operator, we can delay an event action until a stream is silent for a specified amount of time. For example, on the button click, we can set a debounce of 500 milliseconds (half a second). This would run the operation after the button is clicked and then not clicked for half a second:

```
RxView.clicks(button).debounce(500,
        TimeUnit.MILLISECONDS)
```

Unlike debounce which delays the action, the "throttleFirst" operator is used to prevent repeating events within a certain time interval after the first event emitted. ThrottleFirst is useful when it comes to preventing doubling actions when a button is repeatedly clicked, but still applying the action on the first click. For example, use throttleFirst like the following:

```
RxView.clicks(button).throttleFirst(1,
        TimeUnit.SECONDS)
```

The preceding code would allow click events through filtering out any clicks that happen within a second of the first one.

Testing

To fully test our application, we should run a virtual system. Press "Shift+F10" or click the "Run ➤ Run..." menu and select a phone type. You will need to download a system image if you have not already by clicking the "Create New Virtual Device" button and following the wizard. Select a system image and click "Finish".

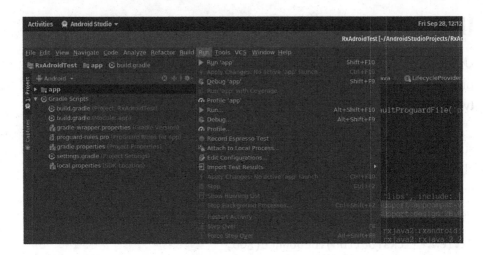

There is much more involved in creating Android applications that is out of the scope of this book.

To learn more, check out a good book or read the online documentation from Google.

CHAPTER 8

Spring Boot and Reactor

Spring Boot greatly simplifies creating a Spring-based application or microservice.

It takes an opinionated approach with sensible defaults for everything you might need and can get you quickly up and running. It uses annotations (no XML needed) and no code generation.

With WebFlux, we can quickly create asynchronous, nonblocking, and event-driven applications using HTTP or WebSocket connections. Spring uses its own Reactive Streams implementation, Reactor (with Flux and Mono), in many of its APIs. Of course, you can use another implementation within your application, such as RxJava if you so choose.

In this chapter, we'll take a look at implementing a full project using Spring Boot, WebFlux, and Reactor with a MongoDB persistence layer.

Getting Started

There are several ways to start a Spring Boot project. Among them are the following:

1. Go to the Spring Initializr and create a project template from there. There are also tools like Spring Tool Suite that take advantage of the spring initializer from your IDE.

2.   Create your own Maven-based project.

3.   Create your own Gradle-based project.

For the purposes of this book, we will choose option three and create a Gradle, Java-based project.

Spring Boot is highly customizable, and you can add whichever "starters" you want for your project (web, mail, freemarker, security, etc.). This makes it as lightweight as possible.

We're going to create a WebFlux-based project that uses Spring's Reactor project along with MongoDB in order to have a fully reactive web application.

The code for this project is available on GitHub at adamldavis/ humblecode.

Gradle Plugin

The most basic Gradle build for Spring Boot with WebFlux looks something like the following:

```
buildscript {
 ext {
  springBootVersion = '2.0.4'
 }
 repositories {
  mavenCentral()
 }
 dependencies {
  classpath("org.springframework.boot:spring-boot-gradle-
plugin:${springBootVersion}")
 }
}
apply plugin: 'org.springframework.boot'
```

```
apply plugin: 'io.spring.dependency-management'
apply plugin: 'groovy'
apply plugin: 'idea'
dependencies { //1
  compile('org.springframework.boot:spring-boot-starter-
  webflux') //2
  compile('org.codehaus.groovy:groovy')
  compileOnly('org.projectlombok:lombok') //3
  compile('org.springframework.boot:spring-boot-starter-data-
  mongodb-reactive') //4
  testCompile('org.springframework.boot:spring-boot-starter-
  test') //5
  testCompile('io.projectreactor:reactor-test') //6
}
```

1. The first thing you might notice is the lack of versions specified; Spring Boot provides those for you and ensures that everything is compatible based on the version of Spring Boot specified. You also don't need to specify the main class. That is determined through annotations.

2. We include the "webflux" starter to enable Spring's WebFlux and "reactor-test" to allow us to test Reactor-based code more easily.

3. We're including Project Lombok here just to simplify the model classes. Lombok gives you annotations that automatically generate boilerplate code like getters and setters.

4. Here we include the Spring Data start for using MongoDB with Reactor integration.

5. We include the "spring-boot-starter-test" artifact to help with our testing of the application.

6. We include "reactor-test" to make testing Reactor-related code easier.

Keep in mind that for the back end to be completely reactive, our integration with the database needs to be asynchronous. This is not possible with every type of database. In this case we are using MongoDB.

At the time of writing, Spring provides reactive integrations "only" for Redis, MongoDB, and Cassandra. You can do this by simply switching "mongodb" for the database you want in the "starter" compile dependency. There is an asynchronous driver available for PostgreSQL, postgres-async-driver, so it might be supported in the future.

Tasks

The Spring Boot plugin adds several tasks to the build.

To run the project, run "gradle bootRun" (which runs on port 8080 by default). Look at the command line output to see useful information like which port your application is running on. For example, the last four lines might be something like the following:

```
2018-09-28 15:23:41.813  INFO 19132 --- [main]
o.s.j.e.a.AnnotationMBeanExporter : Registering beans for JMX
exposure on startup
2018-09-28 15:23:41.876  INFO 19132 --- [server-epoll-13]
r.ipc.netty.tcp.BlockingNettyContext  : Started HttpServer on
/0:0:0:0:0:0:0:0%0:8003
2018-09-28 15:23:41.876  INFO 19132 --- [main]
o.s.b.web.embedded.netty.NettyWebServer  : Netty started on
port(s): 8003
```

```
2018-09-28 15:23:41.879  INFO 19132 --- [main]
c.h.humblecode.HumblecodeApplication : Started
HumblecodeApplication in 3.579 seconds (JVM running for 4.029)
```

When you're ready to deploy, run "gradle bootRepackage" which builds a fat jar with everything you need to run the full application in one jar.

SpringBootApplication

The main class is specified by annotating it with @SpringBootApplication. For example, create a class named HumblecodeApplication and put it in the com.humblecode package and put the following:

```
package com.humblecode;
import org.springframework.boot.SpringApplication;
import org.springframework.boot.autoconfigure.*;
import org.springframework.context.annotation.Bean;
import reactor.core.publisher.Flux;

@SpringBootApplication
public class HumblecodeApplication {

  public static void main(String[] args) { //1
    SpringApplication.run(
        HumblecodeApplication.class, args);
  }
  @Bean
  public Flux<String> exampleBean() { //2
          return Flux.just("example");
  }
}
```

1. The main method calls SpringApplication.run to start the application.

2. Beans can be created directly using the @Bean annotation on methods. Here we create a simple Flux<String> of just one element.

The @SpringBootApplication annotation tells Spring a number of things:

1. To use auto-configuration.

2. To use component scanning. It will scan all packages and subpackages for classes annotated with Spring annotations.

3. This class is a Java-based configuration class, so you can define beans here using the @Bean annotation on a method that returns a bean.

Auto-Configuration

Spring Boot considers the runtime of your application and automatically configures your application based on many factors, such as libraries on the classpath.

It follows the motto: "If everyone has to do it, then why does everyone have to do it?"

For example, to create a typical MVC web app, you will need to add a configuration class and multiple dependencies and configure a Tomcat container. With Spring Boot, all you need to add is a dependency and a controller class, and it will automatically add an embedded Tomcat instance.

Configuration files can be defined as properties files, yaml, and other ways. To start with, create a file named "application.properties" under "src/main/resources" and add the following:

```
server.port=8003
app.name=Humble Code
```

This sets the server to run on port 8003 and sets a user-defined property app.name which can be any value.

Later on you can add your own configuration classes to better configure things like security in your application. For example, here's the beginning of a SecurityConfig class that would enable Spring Security in your application:

```
@EnableWebFluxSecurity
public class SecurityConfig
```

Later on we'll explore adding security to a WebFlux project.

Our Domain Model

For this section, we will be implementing a very simple web site with a RESTful API for online learning. Each course will have a price (in cents), a name, and a list of segments.

We will use the following domain model Course class definition:

```
import lombok.AllArgsConstructor;
import lombok.Data;
import org.springframework.data.annotation.Id;
import org.springframework.data.mongodb.core.mapping.*;
import java.util.*;
@Data //1
@AllArgsConstructor
@Document //2
```

```
public class Course {
 @Id UUID id = UUID.randomUUID(); //3
 public String name;
 public long price = 2000; // $20.00 is default price
 public final List<Segment> segments = new ArrayList<>();
 public Course(String name) {this.name = name;}
}
```

1. The first two annotations are Lombok annotations.
   @Data tells Lombok to add getters and setters
   for every field, a toString() method, equals and
   hashCode() methods, and a constructor.

2. The @Document annotation is the Spring Data
   mongo annotation to declare this class represents a
   mongo document.

3. The @Id annotation denotes the id property of this
   document.

After installing MongoDB, you can start it with the following command:

```
mongod -dbpath data/ --fork \
       --logpath ~/mongodb/logs/mongodb.log
```

ReactiveMongoRepository

First, we need to create an interface to our back-end database, in this case
MongoDB.

Using the spring-boot-starter-data-mongodb-reactive dependency
that we included, we can simply create a new interface that extends
ReactiveMongoRepository, and Spring will generate the code backing any

method we define using a standard naming scheme. By returning Reactor classes, like Flux or Mono, these methods will automatically be reactive.

For example, we can create a repository for Courses :

```
import com.humblecode.humblecode.model.Course;
import org.springframework.data.mongodb.\
repository.ReactiveMongoRepository;
import reactor.core.publisher.Flux;
import java.util.UUID;
public interface CourseRepository extends
ReactiveMongoRepository<Course, UUID> { //1
Flux<Course> findAllByNameLike(String searchString); //2
Flux<Course> findAllByName(String name); //3
}
```

1. The first generic type is the type this repository stores (Course), and the second is the type of Course's ID.

2. This method finds all Courses with the names that match the given search String.

3. This method finds all Courses with the given name. If we were sure names are unique, we could have used Mono<Course> findByName(String name).

Simply by extending the ReactiveMongoRepository interface, our repository will have tons of useful methods such as findById, insert, and save all returning Reactor types (Mono or Flux).

Controllers

Next, we need to make a basic controller for rendering our view templates.

Annotate a class with @Controller to create a web controller. For example:

```
import org.springframework.stereotype.Controller;
import org.springframework.ui.Model;
import org.springframework.web.bind.annotation.*;
@Controller
public class WebController {
  @GetMapping("/")
  public Mono<String> hello() {
        return Mono.just("home");
  }
}
```

As the preceding method returns the string "home" wrapped by a Mono, it would render the corresponding view template (located under src/main/resources/templates), if we have one; otherwise it would just return the string itself.

The GetMapping annotation is identical to using @RequestMapping (path = "/", method = RequestMethod.GET).

By default a WebFlux-based Spring Boot application uses an embedded Netty instance, although you can configure it to use Tomcat, Jetty, or Undertow instead.

Using the embedded container means that container is just another "bean" which makes configuration a lot easier. It can be configured using "application.properties" and other application configuration files.

Next we'd like to add some initial data to our repository so there's something to look at. We can accomplish this by adding a method annotated with @PostConstruct that only adds data to the courseRepository when the count is zero:

```
@PostConstruct
public void setup() {
  courseRepository.count() //1
    .blockOptional() //2
    .filter(count -> count == 0) //3
    .ifPresent(it -> //4
      Flux.just(
      new Course("Beginning Java"),
      new Course("Advanced Java"),
      new Course("Reactive Streams in Java"))
    .doOnNext(c -> System.out.println(c.toString()))
    .flatMap(courseRepository::save) //5
    .subscribeOn(Schedulers.single()) //6
    .subscribe()
); //7
}
```

1. Get the count from the CourseRepository (which has the type Mono<Long>).

2. Call "blockOptional()" which will block until the Mono returns a value and converts the output to an Optional<Long>.

3. Keep the value only if it is zero.

4. If it was zero, we create a Flux of three Course objects we want to save.

5. Map those Courses to the repository's "save" method using flatMap.

6. Specify the Scheduler to use as Schedulers.single().

7. Subscribe the Flux so it executes.

Here the code uses a mix of Java 8's Optional interface with Reactor. Note that we must call subscribe on a Flux or else it won't ever execute. We accomplish this here by calling subscribe() with no parameters.

View Templates

In any Spring Boot project, we could use one of many view template renderers. In this case we include the freemarker spring starter to our build file under dependencies:

```
compile('org.springframework.boot:spring-boot-starter-
freemarker')
```

We put our templates under src/main/resources/templates. Here's the important part of the template file, home.ftl (some is left out for brevity):

```
<article id="content" class="jumbotron center"></article>
<script type="application/javascript">
jQuery(document).ready(HC.loadCourses);
</script>
```

This calls the corresponding JavaScript to get the list of Courses from our RestController which we will define later. The loadCourses function is defined something like the following:

```
jQuery.ajax({method: 'get',
        url: '/api/courses'}).done( //1
  function(list) { //2
    var ul = jQuery(
        '<ul class="courses btn-group"></ul>');
    list.forEach((crs) => { //3
      ul.append(
'<li class="btn-link" onclick="HC.loadCourse(\"+
      crs.id + '\'); return false">'
```

```
      + crs.name + ': <i>' + crs.price + '</i></li>')
   });
   jQuery('#content').html(ul); //4
}).fail( errorHandler ); //5
```

1. First we call our RESTful API, which we will define later.

2. Since we're using jQuery, it automatically determines that the response is JSON and parses the returned data.

3. Using forEach we build an HTML list to display each Course with a link to load each Course.

4. We update the DOM to include the list we built.

5. Here we specify the error handling function in case anything goes wrong with the HTTP request.

Although we're using jQuery here, we could have chosen any JavaScript framework. For Spring Boot, JavaScript files should be stored at src/main/resources/static/js.

RESTful API

By default, Spring encodes data from a @RestController into JSON, so the corresponding CourseControl is defined thusly:

```
import org.springframework.http.MediaType;
import org.springframework.web.bind.annotation.*;
import reactor.core.publisher.*;
import java.util.*;
@RestController
public class CourseControl {
  final CourseRepository courseRepository;
```

```
public CourseControl(
        CourseRepository          courseRepository) {
        this.courseRepository = courseRepository;
}
@GetMapping("/api/courses")
public Flux<Course> getCourses() {
        return courseRepository.findAll();
}
@GetMapping("/api/course/{id}")
public Mono<Course> getCourse(
        @PathVariable("id") String id) {
        return courseRepository.findById(
        UUID.fromString(id));
    }
}
```

Note how we can return Reactor data types like Flux directly from a RestController since we are using WebFlux. This means that every HTTP request will be nonblocking and use Reactor to determine the threads on which to run your operations.

Now we have the ability to read Courses, but we also need the ability to save and update them.

Since we're making a RESTful API, we use @PostMapping to handle HTTP POST for saving new entities and @PutMapping to handle PUT for updating.

Here's how the save method is set to consume a JSON map of values (using a Map just to keep the code simple):

```
@PostMapping(value = "/api/course",
        consumes = MediaType.APPLICATION_JSON_VALUE)
public Mono<Course> saveCourse(
        @RequestBody Map<String,Object> body) {
        Course course = new Course((String)
```

```
            body.get("name"));
        course.price = Long.parseLong(
            body.get("price").toString());
        return courseRepository.insert(course);
}
```

Note that the insert method returns a Reactor Mono instance. As you may recall, a Mono can only return one instance or fail with an error.

The corresponding JavaScript code will be similar to the previous example except the ajax call will be more like the following (assuming "name" and "price" are ids of inputs):

```
var name = jQuery('#name').val();
var price = jQuery('#price').val();
jQuery.ajax({method: 'post', url: '/api/course/',
data: {name: name, price: price}})
```

Here's the update method which will be activated by a PUT request using the given "id" and also expecting a JSON map of values:

```
@PutMapping(value = "/api/course/{id}",
        consumes = MediaType.APPLICATION_JSON_VALUE)
public Mono<Course> updateCourse(
        @RequestParam("id") String id,
        @RequestBody Map<String,Object> body) {
    Mono<Course> courseMono = courseRepository
            .findById(UUID.fromString(id));
    return courseMono.flatMap(course -> {
        if (body.containsKey("price"))
    course.price =
Long.parseLong(
                body.get("price").toString());
```

```
        if (body.containsKey("name")) course.name=
            (String) body.get("name");
        return courseRepository.save(course);
    });
}
```

Note how we use flatMap here to update the course and return the result of the save method which also returns a Mono. If we had used map, the return type would be Mono<Mono<Course>>. By using flatMap we "flatten" it to just Mono<Course> which is the return type we want here.

Further Configuration

In a real application, we will most likely want to override many of the default configurations for our application. For example, we will want to implement custom error handling and security.

First, to customize WebFlux, we add a class that extends WebFluxConfigurationSupport and is annotated with @EnableWebFlux (here the class is named WebFluxConfig, but it could be named anything). Adding that annotation not only tells Spring Boot to enable WebFlux but also to look at this class for extra configuration. For example:

```
import org.springframework.http.HttpStatus;
import org.springframework.web.reactive.config.*;
import org.springframework.web.server.*;
import reactor.core.publisher.Mono;

@EnableWebFlux
public class WebFluxConfig extends WebFluxConfigurationSupport
{
  @Override
  public WebExceptionHandler
            responseStatusExceptionHandler() {
```

```
    return (exchange, ex) -> Mono.create(
      callback -> {
        exchange.getResponse().setStatusCode(
              HttpStatus.I_AM_A_TEAPOT);
          System.err.println(ex.getMessage());
          callback.success(null);
        });
  }
}
```

Here we override the responseStatusExceptionHandler to set the status code to 418 (I'm a teapot) which is an actual HTTP status code that exists. There are many methods that you can override to provide your own custom logic.

Finally, no application would be complete without some form of security. First make sure to add the Spring Security dependency to your build file:

```
compile('org.springframework.boot:spring-boot-starter-
security')
```

Next, add a class and annotate it with EnableWebFluxSecurity from the "org.springframework.security.config.annotation.web.reactive" package and define beans as follows:

```
@EnableWebFluxSecurity //1
public class SecurityConfig {
 @Bean
 public SecurityWebFilterChain
  springSecurityFilterChain(ServerHttpSecurity http){
        http
        .authorizeExchange()
        .pathMatchers("/api/**", "/css/**",
              "/js/**", "/images/**", "/")
```

```
        .permitAll() //2
        .pathMatchers("/user/**")
.hasAuthority("user") //3
        .and()
        .formLogin();
        return http.build();
}
@Bean
public MapReactiveUserDetailsService
        userDetailsService(
                        userRepository) {
        List<UserDetails> userDetails =
            new ArrayList<>();
        userDetails.addAll(
          userRepository.findAll().collectList()
                .block());//4
        return new
MapReactiveUserDetailsService(
                userDetails);
}
@Bean
public PasswordEncoder myPasswordEncoder() { //5
        // never do this in production of course
        return new PasswordEncoder() {
                /*plaintext encoder*/};
}
}
```

1. This annotation tells Spring Security to secure your WebFlux application.

2. We define what paths are allowed to all users using the ant-pattern where "**" means any directory or directories. This allows everyone access to the main page and static files.

3. Here we make sure that a user must be logged in to reach any path under the "/user/" path.

4. This line converts all users from the UserRepository into a List. This is then passed to the MapReactiveUserDetailsService which provides users to Spring Security.

5. You must define a PasswordEncoder. Here we define a plain-text encoding just for demo purposes. In a real system, you should use a StandardPasswordEncoder or, even better, BcryptPasswordEncoder.

The UserRepository would be defined as follows:

```
public interface UserRepository extends
  ReactiveMongoRepository<User, UUID> {}
```

Testing

Spring Boot provides thorough built-in support for testing. For example, annotating a JUnit test class with @RunWith(SpringRunner.class) and @SpringBootTest, we can run integration tests with our entire application running as follows:

```
import org.junit.Test;
import org.junit.runner.RunWith;
import org.springframework.beans.factory.annotation.Autowired;
import org.springframework.boot.test.context.SpringBootTest;
import org.springframework.boot.test.context.\
        SpringBootTest.WebEnvironment;
import org.springframework.boot.test.web.client.\
        TestRestTemplate;
import org.springframework.http.*;
import org.springframework.test.context.junit4.SpringRunner;
import java.util.Arrays;
import static org.assertj.core.api.Assertions.assertThat;
@RunWith(SpringRunner.class)
@SpringBootTest(webEnvironment =
                WebEnvironment.RANDOM_PORT)
public class HumblecodeApplicationTests {
  @Autowired
  private TestRestTemplate testRestTemplate;
  @Test
  public void testFreeMarkerTemplate() {
    ResponseEntity<String> entity = testRestTemplate.
getForEntity("/", String.class);
```

```
    assertThat(entity.getStatusCode())
                        .isEqualTo(HttpStatus.OK);
    assertThat(entity.getBody())
                        .contains("Welcome to");
  }
```

This simple test boots up our Spring Boot application and verifies that the root page returns with HTTP OK (200) status code and the body contains the text "Welcome to". Using "webEnvironment = WebEnvironment. RANDOM_PORT" specifies that the Spring Boot application should pick a random port to run locally on every time the test is run.

We can also test the main function of our application such as the ability to get a list of courses in JSON like the following test demonstrates:

```
@Test public void testGetCourses() {
  HttpHeaders headers = new HttpHeaders();
  headers.setAccept(
        Arrays.asList(MediaType.APPLICATION_JSON));
  HttpEntity<String> requestEntity =
                  new HttpEntity<>(headers);
  ResponseEntity<String> response = testRestTemplate
          .exchange("/api/courses", HttpMethod.GET,
                requestEntity, String.class);
  assertThat(response.getStatusCode())
          .         isEqualTo(HttpStatus.OK);
  assertThat(response.getBody())
    .contains("\"name\":\"Beginning Java\",\"price\":2000");
}
```

CHAPTER 9

Akka HTTP and Akka Streams

When considering which library or framework to use to create a web application making use of Akka Streams, there are many things to choose from, Play Framework, Apache Camel, or Akka HTTP among others. For this chapter, we'll focus on using Akka HTTP. The Akka HTTP server is implemented on top of Akka Streams and makes heavy use of it.

> *Akka HTTP has been driven with a clear focus on providing tools for building integration layers rather than application cores. As such it regards itself as a suite of libraries rather than a framework.*

> –Akka HTTP Docs

Akka HTTP takes an unopinionated approach and prefers to be seen as a set of libraries rather than a framework. Although this can make it more difficult to get started, it allows the developer more flexibility and a clear view of everything that's happening. There's no "magic" behind the scenes that makes it work.

Akka HTTP has support for the following:

- *HTTP*: Akka HTTP implements HTTP/1.1 including persistent connections and client connection pooling.

- HTTPS is supported through the facilities that Java provides.

- *WebSocket*: Akka HTTP implements WebSocket on both the server side and the client side.

- *HTTP/2*: Akka HTTP provides server-side HTTP/2 support.

- *Multipart*: Akka HTTP has modeled multipart/* payloads. It provides streaming multipart parsers and renderers, e.g., for parsing file uploads, and provides a typed model to access details of such a payload.

- *Server-sent events (SSE)*: Supported through marshalling that will provide or consume an (Akka Stream based) stream of events.

- *JSON*: Marshalling to and from JSON is supported out of the box for Jackson-based models in Java.

- Gzip and Deflate Content-Encoding.

It also has a testing library to assist with testing.

For <u>our example project</u>, we'll use Akka HTTP along with Akka Streams and WebSockets to create a real-time chatbot web server with a fake repository.

Getting Started

Although you can use SBT (Scala's build tool), Maven, or many other build tools, here we're using Gradle.

Start by creating a build file named "build.gradle" with the following contents:

```
apply plugin: 'java' //1
apply plugin: 'eclipse'
apply plugin: 'idea'
apply plugin: 'application'
```

```
group = 'com.github.adamldavis'
applicationName = 'akka-http-java' //2
version = '0.0.1-SNAPSHOT'
mainClassName = 'com.github.adamldavis.akkahttp.WebApp' //3
// requires Gradle 4.7+
sourceCompatibility = 1.10 //4
targetCompatibility = 1.10

repositories {
    mavenCentral()
}
ext {
    akkaHttpVersion = '10.1.5' //5
    akkaVersion = '2.5.12'
}
dependencies {
  compile "com.typesafe.akka:akka-http_2.12:$akkaHttpVersion" //6
  compile "com.typesafe.akka:akka-http-jackson_2.12:
  $akkaHttpVersion"
  compile "com.typesafe.akka:akka-stream_2.12:$akkaVersion"

  testCompile "com.typesafe.akka:akka-http-testkit_2.12:
  $akkaHttpVersion"
  testCompile "com.typesafe.akka:akka-stream-testkit_2.12:
  $akkaVersion"
  testCompile 'junit:junit:4.12'
  testCompile "org.assertj:assertj-core:3.11.1"
}
```

1. Specify plugins.

2. Set the application's name.

3. Set the main class with the static void main method
   to run.

4. Set the Java version to 10.

5. Set variables for versions of Akka HTTP and Akka to use.

6. Specify all the dependencies necessary for this project, including the akka-http-testkit, akka-stream-testkit, junit, and assertj for tests.

Then create a class, named WebApp, and start with the following imports:

```
import akka.NotUsed;
import akka.actor.ActorSystem;
import akka.http.javadsl.ConnectHttp;
import akka.http.javadsl.Http;
import akka.http.javadsl.ServerBinding;
import akka.http.javadsl.model.*;
import akka.http.javadsl.server.*;
import akka.stream.ActorMaterializer;
import akka.stream.javadsl.Flow;
import akka.stream.javadsl.Source;
import akka.util.ByteString;
```

Next, make the class extend AllDirectives to enable the Java DSL and add a main method like the following:

```
public static void main(String[] args) {
  ActorSystem system = ActorSystem.create("routes");//1
  final Http http = Http.get(system); //2
  final ActorMaterializer materializer =
      ActorMaterializer.create(system);
  var app = new WebApp(); //3
```

```
final Flow<HttpRequest, HttpResponse, NotUsed>
    routeFlow = app.joinedRoutes()
    .flow(system, materializer);
final CompletionStage<ServerBinding> binding =
    http.bindAndHandle(routeFlow,
            ConnectHttp.toHost("localhost", 5010),
            materializer); //4
System.out.println("Server online at http://localhost:5010/\
nUse Ctrl+C to stop");
// add shutdown Hook to terminate system:
Runtime.getRuntime().addShutdownHook(new Thread(() -> { //5
    System.out.println("Shutting down...");
    binding.thenCompose(ServerBinding::unbind)
            .thenAccept(unbound -> system.terminate());
}));
}
```

1. Create the ActorSystem for this application.

2. Using that system, create an instance of Http, which is the Akka HTTP server.

3. In order to access all directives, we need an instance where the routes are defined.

4. Boot up server, binding it to port 5010 on localhost and using the routeFlow defined in the preceding code.

5. Finally, we add a shutdown hook that unbinds the server and shuts down the ActorSystem.

To run the application, simply use the command "gradle run" at the command line.

Routes

Routes can be defined using the server DSL, with simple names like "route", "path", and "get". The first path matched in your route will cause your handler for that route to be run. If no routes are matched, then a response with HTTP Status 404 (not found) will be returned by default.

For example, the following method defines a route that matches "/hello":

```
private Route createHelloRoute() {
  return route(
        path("hello", () ->
                get(() ->
                  complete(HttpEntities.create(
                  ContentTypes.TEXT_HTML_UTF8,
                  "<h1>Say hello to akka-http</h1>"))
        )));
}
```

This route simply returns a simple HTML entity as seen in the preceding code. We create the HttpEntity by calling HttpEntities.create with a ContentType and String. The "complete" method signifies that the response is completed by the given parameter and is overloaded to take in many different values such as String, StatusCode, HttpEntity, or HttpResponse. It also has a variety with an additional parameter of type Iterable<HttpHeader> to specify the headers of the response. Here we are using the complete(HttpEntity) variety.

The HttpEntities.create method is also overloaded to take a String, ByteString, byte array, path, file, or an Akka Stream Source<ByteString, ?>.

We can test out the route by running our application and then using the "curl localhost:5010/hello" command. We should get the following output:

```
<h1>Say hello to akka-http</h1>
```

Routes can be combined into a single route using the overloaded "route" method allowed for composition of routes. For example:

```java
private Route joinedRoutes() {
  return route(createHelloRoute(),
        createRandomRoute(),
        createWebsocketRoute());
}
```

Here we provide a route combining three routes we define.

Since Akka HTTP is built on top of Akka Streams, we can provide an infinite stream of bytes to any route. Akka HTTP will use HTTP's built-in rate-limiting specification to provide a stream at constant memory use. The following method provides a stream of random numbers for requests on path "/random":

```java
private Route createRandomRoute() {
  final Random rnd = new Random();
  Source<Integer, NotUsed> numbers = //1
  Source.fromIterator(() ->
    Stream.generate(rnd::nextInt).iterator());
  return route(
    path("random", () ->
      get(() ->
        complete(
        HttpEntities.create(
                ContentTypes.TEXT_PLAIN_UTF8,
                numbers.map(x ->
                  ByteString.fromString(x + "\n"))))) //2
      )));
}
```

111

1. Here we use Stream.generate to generate an infinite stream of bytes and then use Source.fromIterator to convert it into a Source.

2. Transform each number into a chunk of bytes using ByteString.

We can test this route using the command "curl --limit-rate 1k 127.0.0.1:5010/random" while the application is running (limits the download rate to 1 kilobyte/second).

WebSockets

Lastly, we can create a WebSocket handling route using "handleWebSocketMessages" like so:

```
public Route createWebsocketRoute() {
  return path("greeter", () ->
    handleWebSocketMessages(
        WebSocketExample.greeter())
  );
}
```

The "greeter" method in WebSocketExample defines a handler that treats incoming messages as a name and responds with a greeting to that name:

```
public static
Flow<Message, Message, NotUsed> greeter() {
  return Flow.<Message>create()
    .collect(new JavaPartialFunction<>() {
      @Override
      public Message apply(Message msg,
                boolean isCheck) {
```

```
      if (isCheck) {
        if (msg.isText()) return null;
        else throw noMatch();
      } else {
        return handleTextMessage(
                msg.asTextMessage());
      }
    }});
}
public static TextMessage
        handleTextMessage(TextMessage msg) {
  if (msg.isStrict()) {
        return TextMessage.create("Hello " +
                msg.getStrictText());
  } else {
        return TextMessage.create(Source.single(
        "Hello ").concat(msg.getStreamedText()));
  }
}
```

The important thing to know about JavaPartialFunction is that it can be called multiple times with isCheck as true or false. If isCheck is true, it is simply checking if your JavaPartialFunction handles the given type, that's why we "throw noMatch()" if the message is not of the TextMessage type (isText returns false).

Testing WebSockets is more complicated because of the complex WebSocket protocol. Next, we'll build a chat application to demonstrate WebSockets in action.

Our Domain

For this example application, we'll build a simple chat server. The core domain model is the ChatMessage as follows:

```java
import com.fasterxml.jackson.annotation.JsonCreator;
import com.fasterxml.jackson.annotation.JsonProperty;
public class ChatMessage {
  final String username;
  final String message;

  @JsonCreator
  public ChatMessage(
        @JsonProperty("username") String username,
        @JsonProperty("message") String message) {
        this.username = username;
        this.message = message;
  }
  // toString, equals, and hashCode omitted for
  // brevity
  public String getUsername() { return username; }
  public String getMessage() { return message; }
}
```

This ChatMessage object is immutable and simply holds the values of the username and message.

We're going to use Jackson for converting to and from JSON, so we've got some annotations to allow this to happen.

Our Repository

For demo purposes, our repository won't actually save but will merely imitate a long-running operation and print out the message that was saved. Its code is as follows:

```
import java.util.concurrent.*;

public class MessageRepository {
  public CompletionStage<ChatMessage> save(
      ChatMessage message) {
  return CompletableFuture.supplyAsync(() -> {
    try { Thread.sleep(500); }
    catch (InterruptedException e)
       { e.printStackTrace(); }
    System.out.println("saving message: " + message);
    return message; });
  }
}
```

It uses Java's CompletableFuture to perform an asynchronous action and sleeps for half a second within that action. In a real application, we'd want to save ChatMessages to some sort of database which potentially would take some time blocking.

ChatServer

The main entry point of the chat server will be the ChatServer class.

It starts with the following imports:

```
akka.NotUsed;
akka.actor.ActorSystem;
akka.http.javadsl.model.ws.Message;
```

115

```
akka.http.javadsl.model.ws.TextMessage;
akka.japi.JavaPartialFunction;
akka.stream.*;
akka.stream.javadsl.*;
com.fasterxml.jackson.databind.ObjectMapper;
org.reactivestreams.Publisher;
java.util.concurrent.*;
```

For brevity we'll skip the fields since they can be derived from the constructor. The ChatServer constructor makes some very important initializations that we'll use to propagate the ChatMessages between the clients:

```
public ChatServer(ActorSystem actorSystem) {
 parallelism =
        Runtime.getRuntime().availableProcessors(); //1
 this.actorSystem = actorSystem;
 materializer = ActorMaterializer.create(
        actorSystem); //2
 var asPublisher = Sink.<ChatMessage>asPublisher(
        AsPublisher.WITH_FANOUT); //3
 var publisherSinkPair =
        asPublisher.preMaterialize(materializer);
 publisher = publisherSinkPair.first();
 sink = publisherSinkPair.second();
 mergeHub = MergeHub.of(ChatMessage.class,
        BUFFER_SIZE).to(sink); //4
 mergeSink = mergeHub.run(materializer);
}
```

1. Here we initialize an int property, parallelism, using
    Java's built-in Runtime class. We set it to the number
    of available processors since that will allow us to
    take advantage of every processor in our parallel
    processing.

2. Create the ActorMaterializer.

3. For brevity we are using Java 10's "var" here as
    the full type is very long. Using the static method
    "asPublisher" on Sink creates a Sink that can also act
    as org.reactivestreams.Publisher. By default it would
    only allow one subscriber, so use WITH_FANOUT
    to allow multiple. We must call preMaterialize to get
    access to the actual instances of Publisher and Sink.

4. Since we want multiple clients to push
    ChatMessages into one sink, we must use
    MergeHub. Much like the previous step, you must
    run the MergeHub with a materializer to gain access
    to the Sink instance.

MergeHub and Publisher

Although it may seem complex, all we've done here using MergeHub and
asPublisher is allow for multiple Flows to use the same Sink that in turn
pushes to an instance of Publisher.

In this way we can have every new WebSocket connection post into
one Sink and subscribe to one central Publisher, as we will see next.

The WebSocket Flow

For our chat-server application, we need to create a main flow. We define it similar to before (with the addition of a Graph) with the following code (some left out for brevity):

```
public Flow<Message, Message, NotUsed> flow() {

Flow<Message, ChatMessage, NotUsed> savingFlow =
  Flow.<Message>create() //1
  .buffer(BUFFER_SIZE, OverflowStrategy.backpressure())
  .collect(new
        JavaPartialFunction<Message,
        CompletionStage<ChatMessage>>() {
  @Override
  public CompletionStage<ChatMessage>
              apply(Message msg, boolean isCheck) {
    if (msg.isText()) {
      TextMessage textMessage = msg.asTextMessage();
      return storeMessageFromContent(
              CompletableFuture.completedFuture(
              textMessage.getStrictText()));
    } else if (isCheck)
      throw noMatch();
    return CompletableFuture.completedStage(
              new ChatMessage(null, null));
  }
  })
  .mapAsync(parallelism, stage -> stage) // 2
  .filter(m -> m.username != null);
final Graph<FlowShape<Message,Message>, NotUsed>graph = //3
```

```
GraphDSL.create(builder -> {
    final FlowShape<ChatMessage, Message>
            toMessage = //4
            builder.add(Flow.of(ChatMessage.class)
            .map(jsonMapper::writeValueAsString)
            .async()
            .map(TextMessage::create));
    Inlet<ChatMessage> sinkInlet =
        builder.add(mergeSink).in(); //5
    Outlet<ChatMessage> publisherOutput = builder
        .add(Source.fromPublisher(publisher)).out();
    FlowShape<Message, ChatMessage> saveFlow =
        builder.add(savingFlow);
    builder.from(saveFlow.out()).toInlet(sinkInlet);//6
    builder.from(publisherOutput)
        .toInlet(toMessage.in()); // 7
    return new FlowShape<>(saveFlow.in(),
        toMessage.out()); // 8
});
return Flow.fromGraph(graph);
}
```

1. Create the Flow. The type declaration describes
    that the Flow takes in a Message and outputs a
    ChatMessage and does not use the supplementary
    data type. We add a buffer with given size, BUFFER_
    SIZE, which could be as big as our system's memory
    could handle. Within the JavaPartialFunction, call
    storeMessageFromContent which we will define later.

2. Unwrap the CompletionStage<ChatMessage> using
    mapAsync. This call allows the database saves to
    be run in parallel using *parallelism* number of
    concurrent threads.

3. Use the GraphDSL to create a FlowShape. This
    Graph will use the preceding savingFlow to save all
    ChatMessages and put them into the mergeSink, but
    use the output from the ChatServer's Publisher so
    that every client gets every ChatMessage.

4. Create the toMessage FlowShape which converts a
    ChatMessage to JSON then wraps it in a TextMessage.

5. Create the "sinkInlet" by adding the mergeSink to
    the Graph's builder. Also create "publisherOutput"
    and "saveFlow" in a similar way.

6. Connect the saveFlow's output to the sinkInlet.

7. Connect the publisherOutput to the toMessage's
    Inlet.

8. Define FlowShape using the Inlet of saveFlow and
    the Outlet of the toMessage Flow.

The helper methods (and fields) such as "storeMessageFromContent"
are defined as follows:

```
private Flow<String, ChatMessage, NotUsed> parseContent() { //1
  return Flow.of(String.class)
        .map(line -> jsonMapper.readValue(line,
                ChatMessage.class));
}
private Sink<ChatMessage, CompletionStage<ChatMessage>>
storeChatMessages() {
  return Flow.of(ChatMessage.class)
        .mapAsyncUnordered(parallelism,
                messageRepository::save) //2
        .toMat(Sink.last(), Keep.right()); //3
}
```

```
CompletionStage<ChatMessage> storeMessageFromContent(
            CompletionStage<String> content) {
  return Source.fromCompletionStage(content) //4
            .via(parseContent())
            .runWith(storeChatMessages(),
                   materializer) //5
            .whenComplete((message, ex) -> { //6
              if (message != null) System.out
                .println("Saved message: "+message);
              else { ex.printStackTrace(); }
            });
}
final MessageRepository messageRepository =
      new MessageRepository();
final ObjectMapper jsonMapper =
      new ObjectMapper(); //7
```

1. The method parseContent returns a Flow that
    converts Strings to instances of ChatMessage using
    Jackson's ObjectMapper, jsonMapper, we define
    later.

2. The method storeChatMessages returns a Sink that
    uses mapAsyncUnordered and the save method
    on messageRepository (allowing saves to occur in
    parallel and in any order).

3. This line materializes the Flow into a Sink that keeps
    only the last element input. This works since it's only
    given a single element.

4. The method storeMessageFromContent starts
    by creating a Source<String> from the given
    CompletionStage<String>.

5. Then, using via(Flow), it converts that String into a ChatMessage.

6. Finally, it uses whenComplete to print out each message that was saved and handles any errors. Although here we just print the stack trace, in a production system, you should either use logging or something else to recover from errors.

7. Create a singleton MessageRepository and ObjectMapper for converting ChatMessages to and from JSON.

We also update the "createWebsocketRoute" method in WebApp to use our new Flow:

```
return path("chatws", () ->
        handleWebSocketMessages(chatServer.flow())
);
```

The Web Client

For the end user to use our WebSocket, we've got to have some kind of front end. For this purpose, we create an "index.html" file under "src/main/resources/akkahttp" with the following content:

```
<!DOCTYPE html>
<html>
<head>
<title>Hello Akka HTTP!</title>
<script>
var webSocket =
  new WebSocket("ws://localhost:5010/chatws"); //1
function submitChat() {
```

```
  var msg = { // 2
    username: document.getElementById("u").value,
    message: document.getElementById("m").value
  };
  webSocket.send(JSON.stringify(msg)); //3
  document.getElementById("m").value = ""; //4
}
webSocket.onmessage = function (event) { //5
  console.log(event.data);
  var content = document.getElementById("content");
  content.innerHTML = content.innerHTML
        + '<br>' +    event.data;
}
</script>
</head>
<body>
 <form> <!--6-->
  Username:<input type="text" id="u"
        name="username"><br>
  Message: <input type="text" id="m"
        name="message"><br>
  <input type="button" value="Submit"
        onclick="submitChat()">
 </form>
<div id="content"></div>
</body>
</html>
```

1. Create the WebSocket connection.

2. Within our "submitChat" function, construct an object named "msg" with a username and message.

3. Send the msg object as a JSON-formatted string.

4. Blank the message input element to communicate to the user that the message was sent and allow a new one to be entered.

5. Define the onmessage event handler of the WebSocket that will append chat messages to the page.

6. Finally, we create the form for the user's input.

Although this is a very simple interface, it is merely to demonstrate the powerful back end. With this simple chat server, we could handle thousands of users at one time.

In a real application, you would improve the interface and add error handling and other features like search, chat rooms, and security.

We also need to update the route to serve this file. Update the *createHelloRoute* method with the following:

```
final Source<String,NotUsed> file =
        Source.single("/akkahttp/index.html");
return route(
  path("hello", () ->
    get(() ->
      complete(
          HttpEntities
            .create(ContentTypes.TEXT_HTML_UTF8,
              file.map(f ->
                WebApp.class.getResourceAsStream(f)) //1
                .map(stream -> stream.readAllBytes()) //2
                .map(bytes -> ByteString.fromArray(bytes))))//3
      )));
```

1. Read the file from the classpath using
    getResourceAsStream.

2. Read all of the bytes from the file using Java's
    InputStream's readAllBytes method.

3. Convert the byte array into a ByteString for
    Akka HTTP.

You can test out the application by running WebApp and visiting
"http://localhost:5010/hello" in several browsers.

Testing

In addition to our standard Akka HTTP and Akka Streams imports, we add
the following imports:

```
akka.testkit.javadsl.TestKit;
akka.util.ByteString;
com.github.adamldavis.akkahttp.*;
org.junit.*;
java.util.*;
java.util.concurrent.*;
static org.assertj.core.api.Assertions.assertThat;
```

The core of our ChatServerTest class is the following setup and
teardown:

```
ChatServer chatServer;
ActorSystem actorSystem;
ActorMaterializer materializer;
@Before
public void setup() {
 actorSystem = ActorSystem.create("test-system"); //1
```

```
chatServer = new ChatServer(actorSystem);//2
materializer = ActorMaterializer.create(actorSystem);//3
}
@After
public void tearDown() {
TestKit.shutdownActorSystem(actorSystem);//4
}
```

1. Before each test we do the following: Create the ActorSystem.

2. Create the ChatServer.

3. Create a ActorMaterializer that we will use for tests.

4. After each test we use the Akka TestKit to shut down the TestKit ActorSystem.

Then we define a test like the following test that simply ensures that a ChatMessage gets copied to the Flow's output as a TextMessage encoded in JSON:

```
@Test
public void flow_should_copy_messages()
throws ExecutionException, InterruptedException {
final Collection<Message> list = new
        ConcurrentLinkedDeque<>(); //1
Flow<Message, Message, NotUsed> flow = chatServer.flow(); //2
assertThat(flow).isNotNull();
List<Message> messages =
  Arrays.asList(TextMessage.create(jsonMsg(0))); //3
Graph<SourceShape<Message>, ?> testSource =
        Source.from(messages);
Graph<SinkShape<Message>, CompletionStage<Done>>
        testSink = Sink.foreach(list::add); //4
```

```
CompletionStage<Done> results = flow.runWith(testSource,
        testSink, materializer).second(); //5
try {
  results.toCompletableFuture().get(2, TimeUnit.SECONDS); //6
} catch (TimeoutException te) {
  System.out.println("caught expected: " +
        te.getMessage());
}
Iterator<Message> iterator = list.iterator();
assertThat(list.size()).isEqualTo(1);

assertThat(iterator.next()
        .asTextMessage().getStrictText())
        .isEqualTo("{\"username\":\"foo\","+
                "\"message\":\"bar0\"}"); //7
}
static final String jsonMsg(int i) {
  return "{\"username\": \"foo\", \"message\": \"bar"
        + i + "\"}";
}
```

1. Create a ConcurrentLinkedDeque (named list) to save the messages to avoid any multithreading issues (this might be overkill).

2. Call flow() to get the WebSocket Flow we want to test.

3. Create a single TextMessage with a JSON-encoded chat message. Although we just create one here, in other tests we could create many using Source.range and then map like the following: Source.range(1, 100).map(i -> TextMessage. create(jsonMsg(i))).

4. Create the testSink which adds each message to our previously defined list.

5. Call flow.runWith with a source, sink, and materializer. This is where the Flow under test is initiated.

6. We must call toCompletableFuture().get on our CompletionStage with a timeout in order to reconnect the current Thread with the test results. Otherwise, it would keep running forever since the underlying Publisher (backed by MergeHub and Sink.asPublisher) has no defined stopping point.

7. Assert that the output TextMessage is encoded to JSON as expected.

The full code on GitHub has many more tests, but this should give you a good idea of how to test an Akka HTTP-based project.

CHAPTER 10

Conclusions

There are many ways one might compare different programming libraries, many of them subjective. Ask ten different programmers and you might get ten different answers.

You might compare libraries' ease of use, size of community, popularity of jobs, flexibility, performance, or some high concept like completeness or cohesiveness, or many other ways. If you do look at performance, keep in mind there are infinite ways to compare performance, and any differences may very well be due to the programmer's limited understanding of these libraries. For the purposes of this book, we will take a short look at each library's unique strengths.

RxJava

RxJava has the benefit of being part of the larger Rx project. If developers are familiar with RxJS, for example, it might be much easier to move to RxJava. It also seems to be the only Reactive Streams library with popular existing open source libraries for building Android applications.

© Adam L. Davis 2019
A. L. Davis, *Reactive Streams in Java*, https://doi.org/10.1007/978-1-4842-4176-9_10

Reactor

Project Reactor is part of the larger Spring Framework suite of libraries. For this reason, it may be more familiar to those who already use Spring, and it has good integration with other projects like Spring Data. With Spring WebFlux, we can very easily create a nonblocking, asynchronous application with a backing MongoDB, Redis, or Cassandra database.

Akka Streams

Akka Streams has the benefit of being part of the larger Akka project. It also has great support in the Scala language. So developers familiar with Scala or Akka in general might find it much easier to work with. It also has the unique concept of Graphs. With Graphs and the related DSLs, programmers can construct large, complex graphs with streams in a way that might be hard to do in the other Reactive Streams libraries.

Conclusion

Any one of these libraries would be a great choice for building reactive, asynchronous, nonblocking, fault-tolerant applications, and the choice of which to use is highly dependent on both the project and the team.

APPENDIX A

Java 10 and 11

Java 10 was released on March 20, 2018. The main substantial update of Java 10 was Local Variable Type Inference (var). It also included enhancements for garbage collection and compilation, but that will not affect how we write our code.

Local Variable Types

Although "var" is not a new keyword, it is a context-sensitive type and represents a huge leap forward for Java developers. It allows you to substitute a type declaration with "var" whenever the type can be clearly inferred from context by the Java compiler.

For example, given a test on our "doParallelSquares" method, we can rewrite it for Java 10+ in the following way:

```
@Test
public void testDoParallelSquares() {
  var result = demo.doParallelSquares()
    .stream().sorted().collect(Collectors.toList());
  assertArrayEquals(squares.toArray(),
        result.toArray());
}
```

Here the type of result is inferred from the right side of the assignment (it happens to be List<Integer>).

© Adam L. Davis 2019
A. L. Davis, *Reactive Streams in Java*, https://doi.org/10.1007/978-1-4842-4176-9

We can use "var" whenever the type is clear from the right side of the assignment, without loss of meaning to human readers. For example, the following is an initialization of a list:

```
var list = new ArrayList();
```

Keep in mind that the type of list will be a raw ArrayList; however, in some cases, that might be fine for our purposes.

With Reactive Streams, it can be helpful to use "var" to simplify code in many cases without losing anything. For example:

```
var monoError = Mono.error(
        new RuntimeException("error")); //1
var foo = Mono.just("foo"); //2
var flux = Flux.just(1, 4, 9); //3
var flux = Flux.just(1);
var stringFlux = flux.map(i -> "string " + i); //4
```

1. Create a Mono that wraps an exception.

2. Create a Mono wrapping a single value.

3. Declare a Flux with initial values.

4. Declare an intermediate step.

Especially in testing, var can useful for simplifying Java code.

```
var publisher = TestPublisher.create(); //1
var stringFlux = publisher.flux(); //2
```

1. Create a TestPublisher from Reactor.

2. Convert it into a Flux.

Lambda Expression Local Variable Types

In Java 11 "var" can also be used in lambda expression parameters for consistency. For example, the following code

```
stringFlux.subscribe(next -> list.add(next), ex ->
ex.printStackTrace());
```

could be changed to the following in Java 11:

```
stringFlux.subscribe((var next) -> list.add(next),
       (var ex) -> ex.printStackTrace());
```

Although a bit longer in syntax, this adds better consistency to the Java language and allows for things like adding annotations to those parameters without specifying a type. For example:

```
stringFlux.subscribe(
       (@NonNull var next) -> list.add(next),
       (@NonNull var ex) -> ex.printStackTrace());
```

We use Java 10+ local variable types throughout the book to simplify some code examples.

Index

© Adam L. Davis 2019
A. L. Davis, *Reactive Streams in Java*, https://doi.org/10.1007/978-1-4842-4176-9

Printed in the United States
By Bookmasters